قد سمعنا ما قلت في الأحلام
The Whisper of Dreams

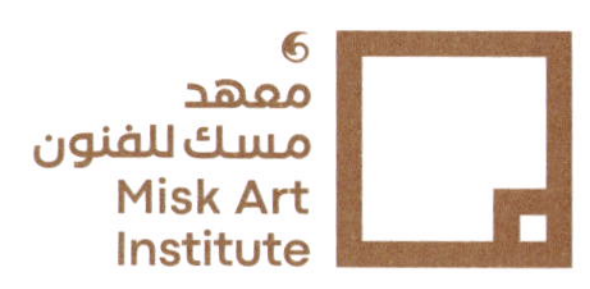

KAPH
ART BOOKS FROM THE ARAB WORLD
كتب الفن من العالم العربي

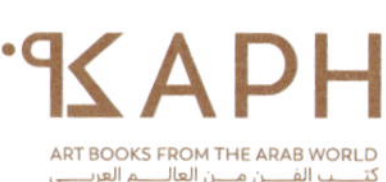

معهد
مسك للفنون
Misk Art
Institute

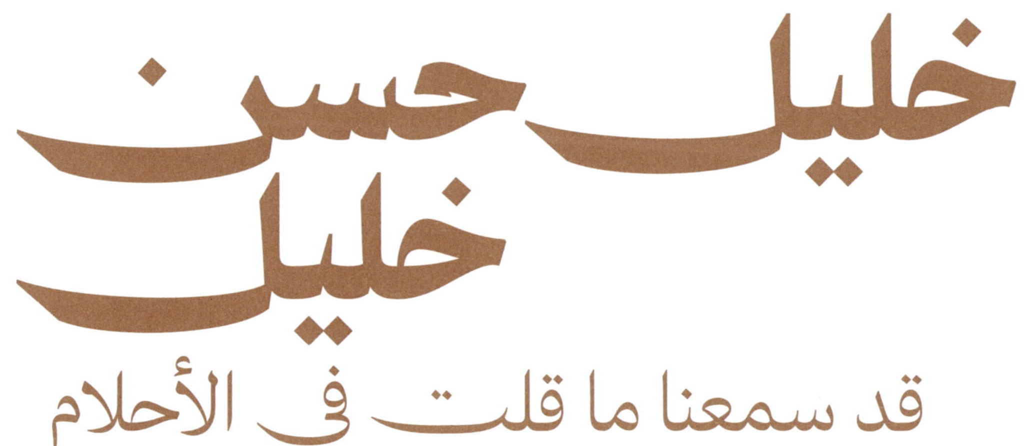

قد سمعنا ما قلت في الأحلام

Khaleel Hassan Khaleel

The Whisper of Dreams

كتيّب المعرض | سلسلة المعارض الفردية
Exhibition Catalog | Solo Series

سلسلة المعارض الفردية
Solo Series

بسمه الشثري، مدير عام إدارة التقييم الفني وكبير القيمين الفنيين

Basma Alshathry, Director of Curatorial Department and Chief Curator

As we embark on the second iteration of Misk Art Institute's Solo Series, we honor the remarkable contributions of two pioneering Saudi artists: Khaleel Hassan Khaleel and Mohammed Alresayes. In this thriving cultural era within the Kingdom of Saudi Arabia, it remains imperative that we document and pay tribute to the influential figures who have significantly shaped our art scene.

The Solo Series continues its mandate to highlight pioneering Saudi artists via a platform for in-depth exploration of their unique creative practices. Khaleel Hassan Khaleel, a painter from Jizan on the Red Sea coast, has developed a distinct approach to his work, which he terms "Dreamism." This approach draws upon his personal and local heritage as a powerful driving force. The thirty-seven works in his solo exhibition, *The Whisper of Dreams*, invite viewers into a dreamlike realm where the boundaries of reality blur, reflecting both the complexities of Khaleel's inner and outer worlds and the rich cultural heritage of his homeland.

Similarly, Mohammed Alresayes's work is deeply rooted in his local Nadji heritage, and he has dedicated his artistic practice to reinterpreting the architectural elements of his hometown. His paintings serve as poignant reminders of the significance of local culture while also nurturing a sense of identity

في النسخة الثانية من «سلسلة المعارض الفردية» التي ينظّمها معهد مسك للفنون، يسعدنا أن نحتفي بفنانين بارزين من أعلام الفن السعودي، خليل حسن خليل ومحمد الرصيص. ففي ظل الحيوية الثقافية التي تشهدها المملكة العربية السعودية اليوم، تبرز أهمية التركيز على الفنانين المؤثرين وتوثيق بصماتهم العميقة في رسم معالم المشهد الفني السعودي وصياغة هويته البصرية المميزة.

تواصل «سلسلة المعارض الفردية» مهمتها في إبراز روّاد الفن السعودي واستكشاف عوالمهم الإبداعية الفريدة، وفي هذا الإطار، يقدّم معرض «قَد سِمعنا ما قُلتَ في الأَحلام» للفنان خليل حسن خليل سبعة وثلاثين عملاً من أعماله، تعكس تأثّره العميق بواقعه، كما تكشف عن فلسفته الفنية الخاصة التي أطلق عليها اسم «الحُلمية»، والتي تستمد إلهامها من التراث الإنساني والعربي، بالإضافة إلى الإرث المحلي لمسقط رأس الفنان -منطقة جازان-. يدعو هذا المعرض الزوّار إلى الانغماس في عالمٍ حُلميّ تتلاشى فيه الحدود بين الواقع والمخيّلة، وتتجلّى فيه الأبعاد النفسية والوجدانية في تفاعل وثيق مع التراث الإنساني والثقافة المحلية الغنية.

وفي إطار آخر، يُقدّم معرض «بين الطراز» عشرين عملاً للفنان الدكتور محمد الرصيص؛ تُظهر مكامن التجذر العميق له في التراث النجدي، وقراءته المعاصرة للعناصر المعمارية التي شكّلت هوية مدينته، ويؤكد الرصيص من خلال أعماله

and continuity with his homeland. Through the twenty works exhibited in his solo exhibition, *Between Forms*, we gain an appreciation for the intricate relationship between architecture and community, as Alresayes captures the essence of his surroundings in a contemporary context.

Both Khaleel and Alresayes, each with their own unique styles, exemplify how local culture profoundly influences creative expression. They embody the spirit of an artistic community that has been instrumental in building a distinct Saudi visual identity. Their works not only contribute to the narrative of the Saudi art scene, but also resonate with universal themes, inviting dialogue and reflection within a broader art historical context.

Misk Art Institute remains committed to preserving and promoting Saudi art history and highlighting its historic figures in order to ensure that future generations can explore and draw inspiration from the rich legacy of Saudi artists. The Solo Series serves as an essential archive that safeguards the vibrancy of the Kingdom's cultural landscape, as we continue to honor the past while looking forward to the future of Saudi artistic expression.

على ثراء الثقافـة المحليـة، ويخلق إحساسـاً بالهوية والانتماء، ويكشف عن العلاقة المترابطة بين العمارة والمجتمـع، سـاعياً إلى إعـادة إحياء ملامـح المكان ضمن سـياق معاصر.

كلا الفنانيـن يقفـان علـى ضفـاف أسـلوبهما الفريد والمختلف، ويقدّمان نموذجاً حيّاً يكشف عن جوانـب تأثير الثقافة المحلية علـى التعبير الإبداعي، ويجسّدان روح الوسط الفني الذي لعب دوراً محورياً في تشـكيل الهوية البصرية السـعودية الأصيلة. كما أن أعمالهمـا لا تقتصـر علـى إثـراء السـردية الفنيـة السـعودية فحسـب، بل تنصت لصدى الموضوعات العالميـة، وتفتح فضاءات للحوار والتأمل في سـياق تاريخ الفن العالمي الأوسـع.

واحتفاءً بتاريـخ الإبداع الفنـي فـي المملكـة، واستشـراقًا للآفـاق الإبداعيـة الواعدة يكـرّس معهد مسـك للفنون التزامه في إبراز هـذا التاريخ والحفاظ عليـه وتسـليط الضـوء علـى روّاده وشـخصياته التاريخيـة، بهـدف تمكيـن الأجيـال القادمـة مـن استكشاف واستلهام هذا الإرث الغني، وتأتي «سلسلة المعارض الفردية» لتسـهم بشـكل فعّـال في توثيق المشـهد الثقافي السـعودي، مُعزّزةً دورها كأرشيف نابـض بالحيـاة يعكـس تطـور الفـن والثقافة فـي المملكة؛ هي بمثابة جسر حي يربط بين إرث الماضي ورؤى المسـتقبل، مسـتعرضةً مسـارات الإبداع التي تشـكل هوية الثقافـة السـعودية المعاصرة.

قد سمعنا ما قلت في الأحلام
The Whisper of Dreams

سيسيليا روجيري وشادن البليهد

Cecilia Ruggeri and Shadin Albulaihed

A pioneering figure in Saudi Arabia's art scene, Khaleel Hassan Khaleel has cultivated a distinctive style and an imaginative vision that have significantly shaped the region's cultural landscape. Thirty-seven of the artist's works are featured in *The Whisper of Dreams*, whose title was inspired by an Abbasid-era poem by Al-Mutanabbi. Highlighting a critical cross-section of paintings, drawings, and preparatory works, the exhibition traces Khaleel's artistic evolution over five decades, from his Impressionist and realist beginnings to the formation of his unique artistic philosophy, which he terms "Dreamism."

Khaleel's practice is rooted in the traditions of his homeland, Jizan, a region renowned for its rich maritime heritage and vibrant natural beauty, located on the Red Sea coast in the southwest corner of Saudi Arabia. From a very young age, he enjoyed comic books about characters such as Batman and Aladdin, which enriched his visual imagination and continue to inform his graphic quality. He would also read *Al-Arabi* magazine's dedicated fine arts page, as it showcased a different artist in each edition (he himself was later featured in the publication). His exposure to art history was further shaped by these readings, along with translated books provided by his teachers, nurturing his early interest in art and culture.[1]

يُعـد خليـل حسـن خليـل أحـد أبـرز الشـخصيات الرائـدة في السـاحة الفنية السـعودية، حيـث ابتكر أسـلوباً مميزاً ورؤيةً واسـعة الخيال ساهمت بشكل ملحوظ في تشكيل المشـهد الثقافي في المنطقة، ويأتـي معـرض «قَد سـمعنا مـا قُلتَ فـي الأحلامِ» ‑المُقتبس عنوانـه مـن إحـدى قصائد أبـي الطيب المتنبـي‑ مقدمًـا قـراءة نقدية لممارسـته لفنيـة، ومسـلطًا الضـوء علـى سـبعة وثلاثيـن مـن أعماله ودراسـاته التحضيريـة، والتـي توضح تطور أسـلوبه منذ بداياتـه الانطباعية وصولاً إلى الفلسـفة الفنية الفريـدة التـي ابتكرَها وأطلـق عليهـا «الحُلمية».

يتجـذّر فنه في الاستقاء من تقاليـد منطقته ‑جـازان‑ الواقعـة علـى سـاحل البحـر الأحمر جنوب غربي المملكة العربية السـعودية، والتي تشتهر بتراثها البحـري الغنـي وجمالهـا الطبيعـي. فمنـذ نعومـة أظفـاره، شـغف خليـل بقـراءة القصـص المصـورة وشـخصياتها، مثل "باتمان" وعلاء الدين، الأمر الذي أثرى مخيلته البصرية وسـاهم فـي تعزيز مهارته في الرسـم؛ كما اعتاد على قـراءة زاوية الفنـون الجميلة من مجلة «العربي» التي كانت تقـدّم وتناقش في كل عدد فناناً مختلفاً، وقد سـاهم هٰذا في تنمية وعيه الفني (وقد اختارته المجلة لاحقًا في أحد أعدادها). إلـى جانب ذلك، لعبت الكتـب المترجمة التي وفرها لـه معلمـوه دوراً أساسـياً فـي توسـيع اطلاعه على تاريخ الفـن وتعزيز إهتمامه بالفـن والثقافة.[1]

---

[1] Khaleel Hassan Khaleel in an interview with the authors; Jizan, Saudi Arabia, January 21, 2025.

[1] خليل حسـن خليـل في مقابلـة مع كاتبـي المقال، جـازان، المملكـة العربية السـعودية، 21 يناير 2025.

After moving to Riyadh to study at the Institute of Art Education, Khaleel began to delve into realism, focusing on refining his ability to depict natural phenomena with precision. After graduating, he explored European museums, traveling extensively across Europe; these experiences exposed him to a myriad of artistic styles and movements of the modernist era. The effects of this period in his life can be seen in his draftsmanship and commitment to realism, even as he imbues it with the absurd. His preparatory studies for these works, a number of which are included in this exhibition, demonstrate his drive to draw anatomical elements from life. Other drawings offer brief initial sketches for a number of compositions and reflect Khaleel's emphasis on the genesis of an idea as central to his practice.

The artist later established his studio in Jizan, where he revisited the ideas and experiences that had shaped his education. Initially, he continued to study natural forms, which he translated into photo-realistic representations. Over time, however, his Impressionist-inspired technique shifted toward a more experimental and conceptual approach.

This transformation marked a departure from traditional aesthetic notions. Central to this evolution was his investigation into the human relationship with machines, which aligned his work with the Dadaist critique of industrialization and its effects on identity and creativity. This theme is evident in works such as *Human and Machine* (1977), in which the artist collates human components with industrial fragments. Drawing inspiration from the intricate composite face series of Giuseppe Arcimboldo (1526–1593), Khaleel adopted a similar approach to create surreal forms that challenge our perception. Like Arcimboldo's portraits—which combine fruits and vegetables, as in *Face* (1977), as well as fish,

حطّت رحال خليل في مدينة الرياض لمواصلة دراسته في معهد التربية الفنية، حيث بدأ بالتعمّق في الأسلوب الواقعي مركّزاً على صقل مهاراته في تصوير الظواهر الطبيعية بدقة. وبعد تخرجه، سافر إلى مدن وعواصم مختلفة في أوروبا، فهناك زار العديد من المتاحف واطلع على مختلف الأساليب والحركات الفنية الحداثية، وتجلّت تأثيرات تلك الفترة من حياته من خلال تخطيطاته التي تُظهر التزامه بالواقعية رغم اللمسة غير المألوفة والمدهشة التي أضفاها عليها؛ ويقدّم المعرض عدداً من رسوماته التحضيرية التي توضح ميله للرسم التشريحي المستمد من الطبيعة مباشرة؛ في حين تُبرز رسوماته الأولية تأكيده على مركزية المنشأ الأول -للفكرة- في ممارسته الفنية.

وقد أسّس لاحقاً مرسمه الخاص في جازان، حيث انكبّ على استكشاف الأفكار والتجارب التي تأثر بها خلال رحلاته ودراساته، وواصل في البداية دراسة الأشكال الطبيعية، والتي ظهرت في أعماله كتمثيلات واقعية قريبة من الصور الفوتوغرافية. ومع مرور الوقت، شهدت تقنيته تحولاً لافتاً، إذ انتقل من أسلوب مستوحى من الانطباعية إلى نهجٍ أكثر تجريبية ومفاهيمية.

شكّل هذا التحول ابتعاداً عن المفاهيم الجمالية التقليدية، حيث انشغل خليل بالنظر في العلاقة بين الإنسان والآلة، ما جعل أعماله تتماهى مع نقد الحركة الدادائية لعصر التصنيع وتأثيره على الهوية والإبداع، ويتجلى هذا الطرح في عدد من اللوحات، مثل لوحة «الإنسان والآلة» (1977م)، التي دمج فيها بين المكونات البشرية والأجزاء الصناعية. واستلهم خليل أيضاً من سلسلة الوجوه المركبة المعقدة للفنان الإيطالي جوزيبي أركيمبولدو (1526-1593م)، متبنياً نهجاً مشابهاً في رسم الأشكال السريالية التي تتحدى الفهم. وكما فعل أركيمبولدو، استخدم الفواكه والخضروات لتشكيل الهيئات البشرية، كما في لوحة «وجه» (1977م)، بالإضافة إلى الأسماك في

seen in *Face (2)* (1978), and other organic materials to form human figures—Khaleel's assemblages laid the foundation for his later works, where his imagery is deeply influenced by Surrealism.

The artist was introduced to Surrealism at an early age, when his middle school teachers gave him a book on Western modern art, marking his first encounter with such works. The Surrealist movement had seminal ramifications in the Arab world,[2] where it spanned political, social, literary, and artistic spheres. It was embraced by a number of Saudi artists, including Abdulhamid Albaqshi, Saleh Khattab, Ahmed Alaraj, and Faisal Mashari, among others. The first wave of Surrealism was the most prevalent among Saudi Surrealists, drawing influences from artists such as Salvador Dalí and Max Ernst. However, as Mohammed Alresayes notes in his publication *History of Fine Arts in Saudi Arabia*, Saudi Surrealist works demonstrate a mature understanding of the movement, blending European influences with local characteristics to create a distinct synthesis.[3]

Khaleel stands out as one of the first Saudi artists to diverge from this direction. His artistic philosophy emphasizes the idea that dreams are not separate from reality; instead, they are an extension of it.[4] His examination of the symbolic realm of dreams reflects the surrealist focus on the imagination and the metaphysical. At the same time, the artist integrates

---

لوحة «وجـه 2» (1978م)، إلى جانب مواد عضوية أخرى، ما أسـس للأسـلوب الذي ميّز أعماله اللاحقة المتأثـرة تأثيـراً كبيـراً بالحركة السـريالية.

يعود تعرّف الفنان على السريالية إلى سن مبكرة مـن حياتـه، عندمـا قـدّم لـه معلمـوه في المدرسة المتوسـطة كتاباً عن الفن الغربي الحديث، فكان ذلك أول لقاء لـه بالأعمال الفنيـة الحداثية؛ تجدر الإشارة إلـى أن الحركة السـريالية تركت أثـراً عميقاً فـي العالم العربي[2]، امتد ليشمل المجالات السياسية، والاجتماعية، والأدبيـة، والفنيـة؛ وقـد تبنى هـذا الاتجاه عـدد من الفنانين السعوديين، ومن أبرزهم عبدالحميد البقشي وصالح خطاب وأحمد العرج وفيصل المشاري. وكانت الموجة الأولى من السريالية الأكثر انتشاراً بين السرياليين السعوديين الذين وعلى الرغم من استلهامهم من كبار السرياليين الغربيين مثل سلفادور دالي وماكس إرنست، إلّا أن أعمالهم تعكس فهماً ناضجاً لهذه الحركة؛ فقد دمجوا التأثيـرات الأوروبية مع الخصائص المحلية، ما أتـاح لهم تطويـر هوية بصرية مميزة، كما يشـير إلى ذلك محمد الرصيص في كتابه «تاريخ الفن التشـكيلي في المملكة العربية السعودية»[3].

يبرز خليل حسـن خليـل كأحد أوائل الفنانين السعوديين الذين ابتعدوا عن السريالية في موجتها الأولـى، مؤكداً في فلسـفته الفنيـة أن «لا تضاد بين الحلـم والواقع بـل الحلم عنـدي امتـداد للواقع»[4]. ويعكـس اهتمامُـه برمزية الأحلام تركيزَه السـريالي على المخيلـة والماورائيات. لكنه في الوقت نفسـه،

2 On the topic of Surrealism in the Arab world, see Stephanie D'Alessandro, *Surrealism Beyond Borders*, exh. cat. (New York: Metropolitan Museum of Art, 2021). The eponymous exhibition was on view at the Metropolitan Museum of Art, New York, from October 11, 2021, to January 30, 2022, and at Tate Modern, London, from February 24 to August 29, 2022. Also see Riad Khardeen, "Surrealism in the Arab World," in *The Routledge Companion to Surrealism*, ed. Kirsten Strom (New York: Routledge, 2022), 165–74. For a specific focus on Egyptian Surrealism, see *Art et Liberté: Rupture, Guerre et Surréalisme en Égypte (1938–1948)*, exh. cat. (Paris: Centre Pompidou, 2016).

3 Mohammed Alresayes, *History of Fine Arts in Saudi Arabia* (Riyadh: Ministry of Culture and Media, Cultural Department, 2010), 189–92.

4 Khaleel Hassan Khaleel and Omar Taher Zaila, *My Dreams* (Jizan: Jizan Literary Club, 1986), 19.

2 عن السـريالية في العالم العربي، انظر إلى ستيفاني داليساندرو، «السريالية خـارج الحـدود»، كتالـوج المعـرض Stephanie D'Alessandro, Surrealism Beyond Borders, exh. Cat. (نيويورك: متحف متروبوليتان للفنون، 2021). أقيم المعرض الذي يحمل نفس الاسم فـي متحف متروبوليتـان للفنون بنيويـورك، مـن 11 أكتوبـر 2021 إلـى 30 يناير 2022، وفـي تيت مودرن بلنـدن، مـن 24 فبرايـر إلـى 29 أغسطس 2022. انظر أيضاً إلـى رياض خاردين، «السريالية في العالم العربي»، في «دليـل روتليدج للسـريالية»، تحرير كيرسـتن سترومRiad Khardeen, "Surrealism in the Arab World," in The Routledge Companion to Surrealism, ed. Kirsten Strom (نيويورك: روتليـدج، 2022)، ص 165-174. للتركيـز بشكل خـاص علـى السـريالية المصرية، انظر إلى «الفن والحرية: الانفصال والحرب والسـريالية في مصر Art et Liberté: Rupture, Guerre et Surréalisme en Égypte (1938-1948)، (1938-1948م)»، كتالـوج المعـرض (باريس: مركـز بومبيدو، 2016).

3 محمد الرصيص، «تاريخ الفن التشـكيلي فـي المملكـة العربية السـعودية» (الريـاض: وزارة الثقافة والإعـلام، القسـم الثقافـي، 2010)، ص 189-192.

4 خليل حسـن خليل، وعمر طاهـر زيلع، كتـاب أحلامي (من إصـدارات النادي الأدبي بجـازان، 1986)، ص19.

توصّل إلى هوية بصرية محلية متفردة، تجاوزت السريالية بحـد ذاتهـا، وأبـدع أعمـالاً تتماشـى مع سـياقه الثقافي والفنـي الخاص.

اسـتلهم خليل أعماله مـن البيئة المحيطة به، مسـتنداً إلى إعـادة تأويـل التراث الإنسـاني والتقاليد الثقافيـة المحلية لبنـاء رمزيته الخاصة، وتتكرر في أعمالـه مجموعـة مـن الرموز التـي تحمـل دلالات عميقـة، كالقمـر والأيـدي والطيـور؛ ولكن الأبـرز بينهـا هو البحـر وعناصـره، مثل الأصداف والمحار والقـوارب، التي تظهـر فـي لوحاتـه بشـكل متكـرر كموضوعـات أو مكونات رئيسـية.

يمثل البحر أسـطورة عميقة التجذر في التراث البحري الغنـي في منطقة جازان -موطـن الفنان- حيـث يمتزج نسـيم البحـر العليـل بأهازيـج البّحارة وحكاياتهـم، وقد ارتبطت صناعـة القوارب والملاحة والفولكلـور البحري ارتباطاً وثيقاً بماضي جازان التي كانت مركزاً بارزاً لاسـتخراج اللؤلـؤ في البحر الأحمر[5]. ويتجلى هذا الإرث البحري بوضوح في أعمال خليل، مثل لوحتي «النهاية» (1977م) و«البحر» (1981م)؛ وكلاهما تتضمنان إشـارات مباشـرة إلـى البحـر، الذي يجـاوره أشـكالاً مختلفـة تعطـي لأعمالـه رمزيـات متعـددة كالأيدي والبيض والطيـور البحرية، ليدمج خليل هذه الرموز في سـياقات غيـر متوقعة تضفي على أعماله طابعاً سـريالياً شـبيهاً بالأحلام.

يلاخظ الترابط الوثيق في ما بين جميع الرموز ضمن أعمال خليل، وانسجامها مع موضوعاته الفنية الكبـرى، فمن خـلال تأمل الرموز عبر لوحاتـه، يمكن استشـفاف العديد من التفسيرات. غيـر أن البرتقال، على سـبيل المثـال، يحمل معنـى محـدداً ومتفرداً، فعلـى عكـس الرمـوز الأخـرى التـي تتسـم بالمرونة

---

a distinct local identity that goes beyond the movement itself, creating works that deeply resonate with his cultural and artistic context.

Drawing inspiration from his surrounding environment, Khaleel built his symbolism by reinterpreting both human heritage and local cultural traditions. Recurring symbols in his work include the moon, hands, birds, and, most prominently, the sea and its elements: seashells, oysters, and boats, which frequently appear as central themes or components in his paintings.

The sea represents a mythology deeply rooted in his homeland's rich maritime heritage, with its enchanting sea breezes and voices of sailors. Boatbuilding, navigational practices, and sea folklore are intertwined with Jizan's past as a prominent center of the Red Sea's pearling industry.[5] This is particularly evident in paintings such as *The End* (1977) and *The Sea* (1981), both of which incorporate direct symbolic references to the ocean, in addition to uncanny symbols that recur in Khaleel's works, such as hands, eggs, and seabirds. Khaleel incongruously places these elements in contexts that give his works their surreal, dreamlike qualities.

All of the symbols in Khaleel's works are interconnected and woven into the overarching themes of his art; translated across different works, they begin to imply multiple interpretations. Oranges, however, hold a uniquely specific meaning. Unlike the artist's other motifs, which are broadly symbolic, oranges serve as direct representations of life itself. His fascination with them began when he noticed the

5   لمزيـد من المعلومات حـول الماضي البحري لجازان، انظر إلى ديونيسـيوس أجيوس وجون كوبر ولوسـي سـمعان وكيارا زازارو وروبرت كارتر، «تذكر البحر: ذكريـات شـخصية وجماعيـة عـن الحيـاة البحرية في جـازان وجزر فرسـان، المملكة العربية السـعودية»، مجلة الآثـار البحرية، المجلـد 11، العـدد 2 (أغسطس 2016)، 127-177. Dionisius A. Agius, John P. Cooper, Lucy Semaan, Chiara Zazzaro, and Robert Carter, "Remembering the Sea: Personal and Communal Recollections of Maritime Life in Jizan and the Farasan Islands, Saudi Arabia," Journal of Maritime Archaeology, vol. 11, no. 2 (August 2016): 127-77, https://link.springer.com/article/10.1007/s11457-016-9159-2.

5   For more on Jizan's maritime past, see Dionisius A. Agius, John P. Cooper, Lucy Semaan, Chiara Zazzaro, and Robert Carter, "Remembering the Sea: Personal and Communal Recollections of Maritime Life in Jizan and the Farasan Islands, Saudi Arabia," *Journal of Maritime Archaeology*, vol. 11, no. 2 (August 2016): 127-77, https://link.springer.com/article/10.1007/s11457-016-9159-2.

intricate beauty of a half-eaten orange—the texture of its peel, the arrangement of its seeds, and its internal structure—prompting him to sketch it immediately. Over time, such observations transformed into metaphorical allusions to vitality and existence, making the orange a distinctive and personal symbol within his signature style.

Referring to his style as "Dreamism," a term he coined in the 1980s, Khaleel draws inspiration from Surrealist techniques, particularly the "Exquisite Corpse"[6] method, by which a collection of words or images is assembled. He thereby adopts the movement's sense of freedom and its visual language of absurdity. However, Khaleel's work diverges significantly from the themes of the Surrealist movement, which often centered on desires, Freudian theories, and psychoanalysis. Instead, his art is rooted in reality and tackles social, humanitarian, and political issues, including wars and historical events, which the artist reinterprets through his distinct perspective.

Khaleel derives his subject matter by reimagining human heritage and reinterpreting local cultural traditions, including pre-Islamic literature and poetry, in particular. This is evident in works such as *The Fall of Granada* (1982), which explores the symbolic loss of the last Muslim stronghold, or *The Third Night After Thousand* (1980), which reinterprets the story of *One Thousand and One Nights*, a central text of Arab culture. Through the symbol of the rooster and the abstracted female body, Khaleel critiques how, since the Ottoman Empire, the role of women in society has been continuously diminished and reduced.

What sets Khaleel apart from other artists is his symbolic approach to presenting subjects,

الدلالية، استخدم الفنان صورة البرتقال كتمثيل مباشر للحياة نفسها، وقد بدأ شغفه بها عندما لفت انتباهه الجمال المعقد لبرتقالة نصف مأكولة، حيث أدهشه ملمس قشرتها، وترتيب بذورها، وبنيتها الداخلية؛ ما دفعه إلى رسمها على الفور. ومع مرور الوقت، تحولت مثل هذه الملاحظات البصرية إلى إشارات مجازية تعكس مفاهيم الحيوية والوجود، ما جعل البرتقال في أعماله رمزاً شخصياً متفرداً، يحمل بعداً فلسفياً خاصاً به.

يشير خليل إلى أسلوبه بمصطلح «الحُلمية»، وهو مصطلح صاغه في ثمانينيات القرن العشرين، مستلهماً من تقنيات السريالية، وخاصة مفهوم «الجثة الرائعة»[6] – وهي ممارسة فنية جماعية، يساهم كل مشارك فيها برسم أو كتابة شيء دون معرفة ما أضافه الآخرون، وبهـذا تبنّى خليـل حرية السريالية ولغتها البصريـة العبثية، ولكنه في الوقت نفسه ابتعد عن موضوعاتها الرئيسـية التي غالباً ما ركّزت على الغرائز والنظريـات الفرويدية والتحليل النفسـي. وعوضاً عن ذلك، جذّر فنّه في الواقع، متناولاً القضايا الاجتماعية والإنسـانية والسياسـية، بما فيها الحـروب والأحداث التاريخية، التي أعاد تفسـيرها مـن منظوره الخاص.

ويستمد خليل موضوعاته من إعادة تصور التراث الإنساني وإعادة تأويل التقاليد الثقافية المحلية، مع تركيز خاص على الأدب والشعر الجاهلي، ويتجلى هذا التوجـه بوضوح فـي لوحات مثل «سـقوط غرناطة» (1982م)، التي تتناول الخسـارة الرمزية لآخر معقل للمسـلمين فـي الأندلس، ولوحـة «الليلة الثالثة بعد الألـف» (1980م)، التي تعيد قراءة قصص «ألف ليلة وليلـة» ذات الأهميـة المحوريـة في الثقافة العربية، ومـن خلال توظيفـه لرمـوز الديك والجسـد الأنثوي التجريـدي، قدّم نقـداً بصريـاً لتقليـص دور المرأة في المجتمع منـذ العهد العثماني.

مـا يميز خليـل عـن غيره مـن الفنانيـن هـو نهجـه الرمـزي فـي تقديـم الموضوعات، مسـتلهماً

drawing inspiration not only from Surrealism, but also from art history, more broadly. While his work is most clearly influenced by Salvador Dalí, Khaleel incorporates elements from a variety of artists. This is particularly evident in his painting *Night* (1979) (figs. 1 and 2), where he borrows and reinterprets a figure from Eugène Delacroix's *Women of Algiers in Their Apartment* (1834), adding a traditional *daffa* (tambourine), typically used in traditional dances performed in Jizan.

When Khaleel painted *Night*, he was just eighteen years old. He reinterpreted the black figure from Delacroix's painting in a way that parallels Pablo Picasso's approach in his 1955 series *Les Femmes d'Alger (Women of Algiers)*. For Khaleel, this reinterpretation is not merely a matter of borrowing motifs; it is about reconceptualizing them in a global art historical framework. Moreover, the symbols he adopts are transformed rather than directly quoted, blending his own elements with classical influences through carefully reconstructed relationships between familiar motifs. For example, the body with the instrument in *Night* later appeared in Khaleel's painting *Sindabad* (1982), evolving into a recurring motif that became part of his visual vocabulary.

In a more recent work, *Sulamaniya Time* (2011), the artist again draws inspiration from Jizan's cultural heritage. This time, he pays homage to the hour before sunset, known as a time of quiet reflection and meditation. The painting features a clock with an orange at its center, symbolizing the stillness of this moment, inspired by Khaleel's childhood memories of lively salons falling silent as the Sulamaniya hour arrived. The motifs that have guided Khaleel's practice over the decades reappear: the sea in the background; the organic, amorphous forms that seem almost fleshlike, framing the abstracted clock; and the ever-present orange, the symbol of life.

مـن السـريالية من جانـب، وتاريخ الفـن على نطاق أوسـع من جانب آخر، وعلى الرغم من تأثره الواضح بسـلفادور دالي، فإنه يسـتعير عناصر مستوحاة من مجموعة متنوعـة من الفنانين؛ يتضح ذلك بشـكل خاص في لوحته «الليل» (1979م) (الشكلان 1 و2)، حيـث اسـتعار وأعـاد تقديم شـخصية مـن لوحة «نسـاء جزائريـات فـي شـقتهن» (1834م) للفنـان الفرنسـي أوجين ديلاكروا، مضيفاً إليها عنصراً بصرياً محليـاً يتمثـل في الـدف التقليـدي الذي يُسـتخدم عـادةً في الرقصـات التراثيـة التي تُؤدى فـي جازان.

كان خليل في الثامنة عشـرة مـن عمره عندما رسـم لوحة «الليـل» التـي أعاد فيهـا تشـكيل المرأة السـوداء من لوحة ديلاكروا بطريقة تتـوازى مع ما قـام بـه بابلو بيكاسـو فـي سلسـلته «نسـاء الجزائر» التي رسـمها عـام 1955م. لكـن في نظـر خليل، لم تكن إعادة التشكيل مجرد استعارة للعناصر البصرية، بل إعادة تصور ضمن إطـار تاريخي فني عالمي، من حيث إنه لا ينسخ العناصر والتأثيرات الكلاسيكية التي يسـتعيرها، بل يعمل علـى تحويلها وإعـادة تركيبها بعناية. فعلى سـبيل المثـال، تعود الشـخصية التي تحمـل آلة الطـرب في لوحـة «الليـل» إلـى الظهور لاحقـاً فـي لوحة «سـندباد» (1982م)، متحولة إلى عنصر متكرر شكّل جزءاً من مفردات الفنان البصرية.

فـي إحـدى لوحاتـه الأحـدث، «السـاعة السـليمانية» (2011م)، يعـود خليل مـرة أخرى إلى التـراث الثقافـي لجـازان؛ مسـتحضراً لحظـة زوال الشـمس والانتقال من النهار إلى الليل، وهي سـاعة التأمل والسكينة. تُصور هذه اللوحة ساعة تتوسطها برتقالة، ترمز إلى هدوء هـذه اللحظة الفاصلة. وقد استوحاها الفنان من ذكريات طفولته عن المجالس التـي كانت تضجّ بالحيـاة قبـل أن يختيّـم عليهـا الصمـت مع حلول السـاعة السـليمانية تجمع هذه اللوحـة بيـن أبرز العناصـر التي ميزت مسـيرة خليل الفنيـة علـى مـدى العقـود، حيـث يظهـر البحر في الخلفية، إلى جانب الأشـكال العضويـة الغريبة التي تشـبه الأجسـاد، والتي تؤطر الساعة التجريدية، فيما تظـل البرتقالة، رمـزّ للحياة، وعنصراً دائـم الحضور.

Khaleel Hassan Khaleel's work is a synthesis of local heritage, surrealist imagination, and symbolic storytelling. By reinterpreting traditional motifs and exploring universal themes, he has developed a distinct visual language that challenges perception while honoring his roots. His unique approach, exemplified by his concept of Dreamism, reflects a deep engagement with cultural identity, history, and the human condition. *The Whisper of Dreams* celebrates Khaleel's legacy, offering an intimate look at how his art transcends cultural and artistic boundaries to weave local, personal, and global histories.

وتُعتبر أعمال خليل حسن خليل بوتقة ينصهر فيهـا التراث المحلـي والمخيلة السـريالية والقصص الرمزية، وقد اسـتطاع الفنان من خلال إعادة تفسير العناصر البصرية التقليدية واستكشاف الموضوعات العالمية، أن يطور لغـة بصرية متفـردة تتحـدى الفهـم وتحتفي بجـذوره في آن واحـد. وتعكس مقاربته الفريدة، التي تتجلى في مفهوم «الحُلمية»، التزامـه العميـق بالهويـة الثقافية والتاريخ والحالة الإنسانية. وبذلـك يحتفي معرض «قـد سـمعنا ما قُلـت فـي الأحـلام» بهـذا الإرث الـذي تركه خليل، ملقياً نظرة حميمة على كيفية تجاوز فنه للحدود الثقافيـة والفنيـة، لنسـج تاريـخ يجمـع بيـن البعد المحلي والشـخصي والعالمي.

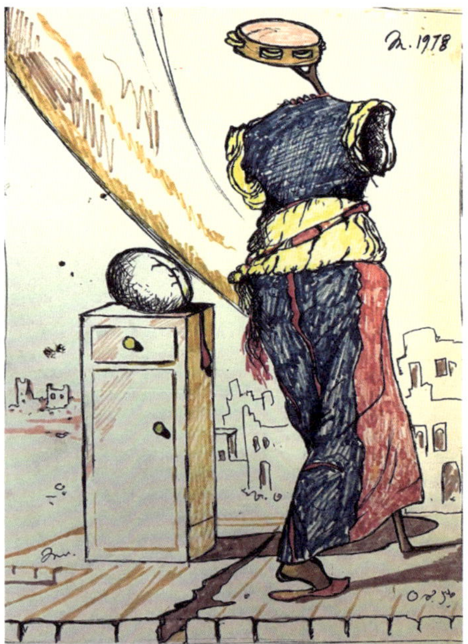

figs. 1 and 2

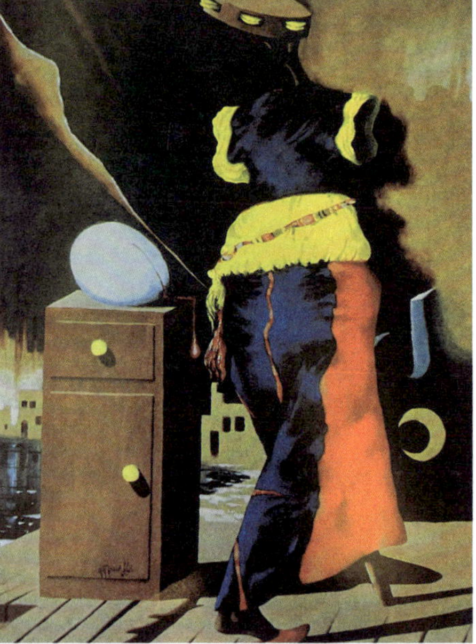

الشكلان 1 و2

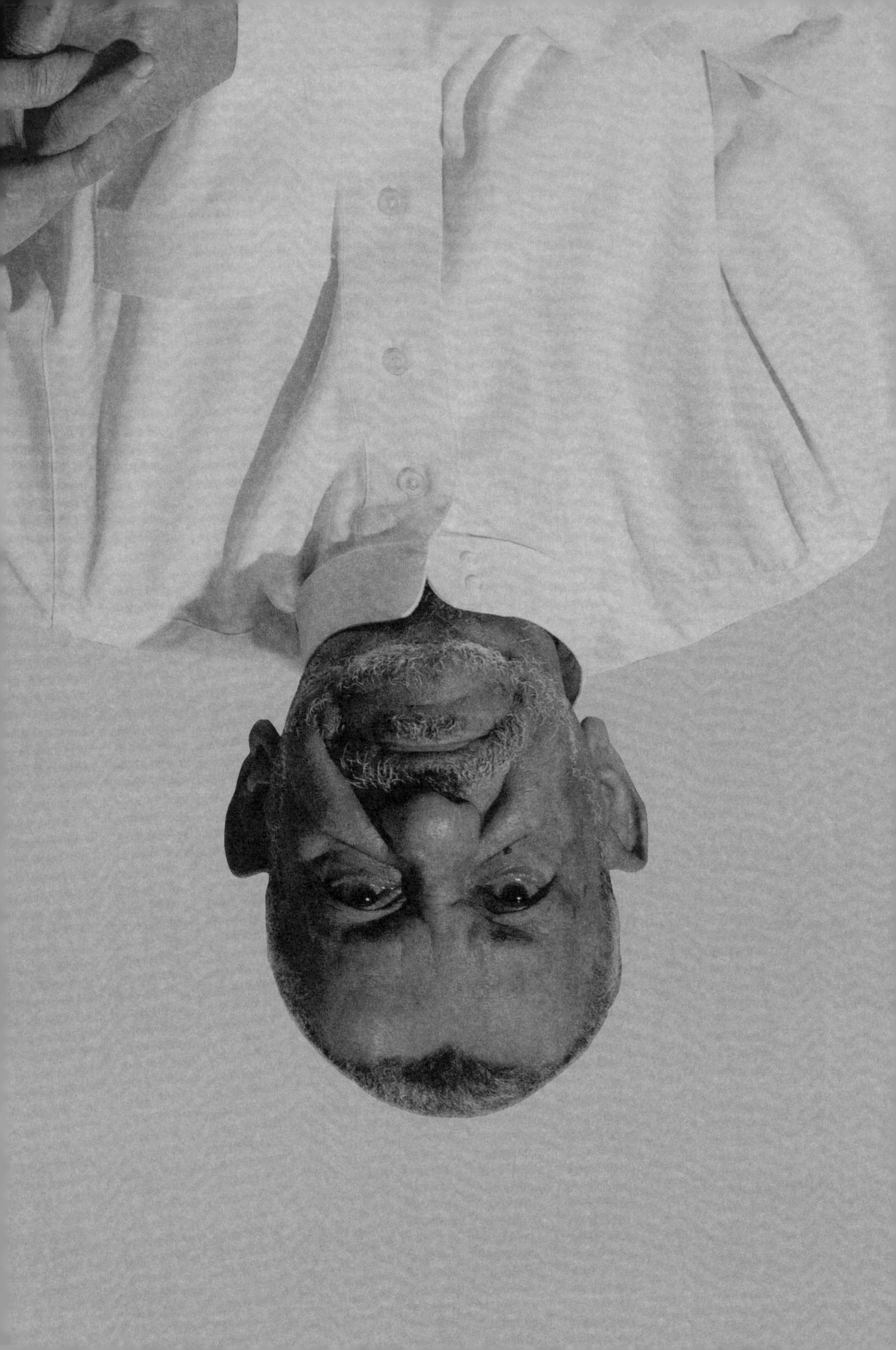

خليل حسن خليل
Khaleel Hassan Khaleel

من مواليد 1958م في جازان، المملكة العربية السعودية
b. 1958, Jizan, Saudi Arabia

سيسيليا روجيري وشادن البليهد
Cecilia Ruggeri and Shadin Albulaihed

Renowned for his distinctive artistic style, Khaleel Hassan Khaleel has established himself as a pioneer in the art scene of Saudi Arabia. He has also played a significant role in the artistic development of Jizan, the region where he was born. The painter graduated from the Institute of Art Education in Riyadh in 1976, and thereafter, he returned to Jizan to teach art at a local middle school. He obtained a diploma in art education from the Intermediate College for Teachers in Madinah.

In his hometown, Khaleel attended King Saud Elementary School, where his talent became evident early on. He was deeply influenced by his childhood art teachers, one of whom encouraged him to draw from his imagination rather than his surroundings. For instance, his middle school Sudanese art teacher, Mohammad Badr Al-Din Hassan, greatly encouraged his talent. His father also supported his artistic endeavors; Khaleel held his first exhibition in his parents' courtyard after completing middle school. Beyond his formal education, he found inspiration in his first encounter with a painting by pioneer artist and educator Abkar Omar Salem (b. 1940), who had made significant contributions to the advancement of fine arts in Jizan. Salem provided

خليل حسـن خليل، هـو أحـد أعـلام الفن التشـكيلي في المملكة العربية السـعودية، عُرف بأسـلوبه الفني المتفـرّد الذي رسّـخ مكانته كأحـد كبار رواد الحركة الفنية في المملكة، وقد لعب دوراً محورياً في تطور الفن في مسقط رأسه -منطقة جازان-. تخرّج خليل من معهد التربية الفنية بالرياض عام 1976م، ليعود بعدها إلى جـازان مبتدئاً مسـيرته المهنية كمدرّس للفـن فـي إحـدى المـدارس المتوسـطة المحليـة، وحصـل لاحقًـا علـى دبلـوم فـي التربيـة الفنية من الكلية المتوسطة لإعداد المعلمين بالمدينة المنورة.

درس خليل المرحلـة الابتدائيـة فـي مدرسـة الملـك سـعود بجازان، حيـث برزت موهبتـه الفنية فـي سـن مبكـرة، وحظـي بدعـم وتشـجيع معلميه، الذيـن حفّـزوه علـى الإبـداع والتعبيـر مـن خيالـه بـدلاً مـن الاكتفـاء بتصويـر محيطـه. وفـي المرحلة المتوسـطة، تبنّى موهبتّه أستاذه محمد بدر الدين حسـن، معلم الفن السـوداني، الذي كان له دور كبير فـي صقل مهاراتـه، وكان لوالـده كذلـك دور بـارز فـي رعايـة موهبته، حيـث أتاح لـه الفرصة لإقامة معـرض فنـي فـي فنـاء منـزل العائلـة بعـد إكمالـه المرحلة المتوسـطة. وإلـى جانب تعليمه الرسـمي، تأثر الفنان بشـكل خاص حين وقعت عينه علـى أول لوحـة أصليـة مرسـومة بالألـوان الزيتيـة، وهي من إبـداع الفنان الرائد الأسـتاذ أبكر عمر سـالم (مواليد

1940م)، الذي تـرك بصمة مؤثرة في تطور الفنون التشـكيلية في جـازان. وحظـي خليل بفرصـة تلقيه لبعـض التوجيهـات القيّمة منـه، والتـي كان لها أثر بالغ فـي مسـيرته الفنية.

وعلـى مـر السـنين، شـهدت أسـاليب خليـل وتقنياتـه الفنيـة تطـوراً لافتـاً، فخـلال دراسـته في معهد التربية الفنية، انجذب إلى المدرسة الواقعية، مقتنعـاً بـأن جوهر الفن يكمن في محـاكاة الطبيعة بأمانـة. إلا أنه سـرعان ما تبنّى الانطباعيـة، محافظاً على لمسـة واقعية. واسـتلهم من الفنـان الهولندي بييـت موندريـان مـا جعلـه يخـوض لفتـرة وجيـزة فـي عالـم التجريـد الهندسـي، قبـل أن يتجـه إلـى المنهجية الدادائية، وتمحورت أعماله المبكرة، التي اتسـمت بأسـلوب الكـولّاج الدادائـي، حـول التفاعل بين العلاقات الإنسـانية والآلات. ومـع مرور الوقت، اتّسـعت رؤيته الفنية لتشـمل موضوعات مستوحاة مـن التـراث العربـي والمحلـي، إلـى جانـب البيئـة الطبيعيـة، وصـولًا إلـى ذروة تطـوره الفنـي، حيث تبنّى مقاربـة سـريالية للواقعيـة، أطلق عليها اسـم «الخُلمية». ويتميّز هذا الأسلوب الفريد بتركيبات غير مألوفة تمـزج بين العناصر الواقعية والسـيناريوهات الشـبيهة بالأحلام، في استكشـاف عميـق لتعقيدات النفس البشـرية ومشـاعرها الإنسـانية.

غالباً مـا تثير لوحـات خليل إحساسـاً بالارتباك بسـبب ألوانها الداكنة وصورها المقلقة وموضوعاتها التـي تغـوص في تعقيـدات التوتـر والتحـوّل، حيـث تندمج الهيئات البشرية مع عناصر مختلفة ، فنجدها تـذوب فيهـا أو تتحـوّل إليها. ونلاحظ في أعماله تكرار لصورة البحـر أو الأيـدي أو البرتقـال، هذا التكـرار له دلالاته الرمزية الغامضـة التي تفتح أُفق التأويل أمام المتلقي. وتجدر الإشـارة إلى أن خليل يسـتقي رؤيته الفنية من جذوره الثقافية، حيث تستلهم أعمالُه من تراث منطقته ومن الموروث العربي، كما تغوص في أعمـاق المخيلة البشـرية، متناولـةً قضايـا اجتماعية وسياسية عبر تصاوير رمزية بارعة، وتكوينات تشكيلية مبتكرة، ومسـتويات متباينة من الواقعية.

Khaleel with invaluable creative guidance that left a lasting impact on his career.

Over the years, Khaleel's artistic journey evolved significantly in both style and technique. During his time at the Institute of Art Education, he was initially drawn to realism, believing that art's essence lay in faithfully replicating nature. Later in his studies, however, he embraced Impressionism while maintaining a foundation in realism. Inspired by Piet Mondrian, he also briefly explored geometric abstraction before transitioning to Dadaist approaches. These early works, reminiscent of Dadaist collages, reflected his interest in the interplay between human relationships and machines. His practice expanded over time to encompass themes inspired by Arab and local heritage as well as the natural environment, ultimately culminating in a surrealistic approach to realism, which he refers to as "Dreamism." This unique style is characterized by unconventional compositions that blend tangible elements with dreamlike scenarios, exploring the complexities of human emotions and the psyche.

His paintings therefore often evoke a sense of unease through dark tones and unsettling imagery, delving into themes of tension and transformation, where human forms merge with or dissolve into other objects. Deeply rooted in his region's cultural heritage and inspired by his surroundings and Arab traditions, Khaleel's works delve into the human imagination as they address social and political issues. He deftly renders symbolic depictions through inventive compositions and varying levels of graphic realism. In his practice, recurring motifs, such as the sea, hands, and oranges, carry layered and ambiguous connotations.

A defining feature of his style is a strong graphic quality that lends his subjects a sense of visual dynamism and intensity. Whether portraying landscapes, human figures, or surreal amalgamations, Khaleel's graphic approach imbues each element with a tangible presence. In contrast, some of his works incorporate softer, smudged brushwork that introduces an ethereal, dreamlike quality.

Nearly a decade after establishing his private studio in Jizan in 1977, Khaleel held his first solo exhibition at the Jizan Literary Club. That same year, the club published a book of his works titled *My Dreams* (1986) with accompanying essays. His second solo exhibition, organized by the Saudi Arabian Society for Culture and Arts, was held in Abha in 1988.

The artist has participated extensively in group exhibitions, starting locally with *The Contemporary Saudi Art Exhibition* in Riyadh (1979), followed by *The Great Saudi Exhibition* (1980) in Riyadh. He was also part of the second group exhibition at the International Gallery in Riyadh, which was organized by the Saudi Art House (1981), as well as the inaugural exhibition of the Saudi Arabian Society for Culture and Arts branch in Jizan (2002).

Internationally, Khaleel has taken part in *The Cultural Week of the Gulf Cooperation Council Countries*, Paris, France (1981); *The Contemporary Saudi Art Exhibition*, Bonn, Germany (1981); and the *International Exhibition for Energy*, New York, USA (1981). Additionally, he was part of the *Seventh Kuwait Exhibition for Arab Artists*, Kuwait City, Kuwait (1981); *The Contemporary Saudi Art Exhibition*, Amman, Jordan (1982); the *Arab Youth Festival*, Baghdad, Iraq (1982); the *Saudi Art Cultural Week*, Morocco, and the *Arab Cultural Week*, Sweden (1983); *The Eighth Kuwait Exhibition for Arab Artists*, Kuwait City, Kuwait (1983); and the eighteenth *International Prize for Contemporary Art* exhibition at the National Museum of Monaco in Monte Carlo, Monaco (1984).

يتميّـز أسـلـوب خليـل بحرفيّـة اسـتثنائية فـي الرسم، إذ تمنح لوحاته إحساساً بالتوهّج والديناميكية البصريـة سـواءً فـي تصويـر المناظـر الطبيعيـة، أو الأشـكال البشـرية، أو التكوينـات التخيّليـة، فإنـه يضفـي علـى كل عنصـر مـن عناصـر اللوحـة حضوراً واقعيـاً ملموسـاً نابضـاً بالحيـاة، وعلـى النقيض من هذا الوضوح الحسـي، تتضمّن بعـض أعماله ضربات ناعمـة بالفرشـاة ، تسـبغ عليها طابعـاً أثيريـاً حالمـاً.

بعد قرابة عقد من الزمان على تأسيس مرسمه الخاص فـي جـازان عام 1977م، أقـام خليل معرضه الفـردي الأول فـي نـادي جـازان الأدبي، وفـي العام نفسـه، أصدر لـه النـادي كتابـاً بعنـوان «أحلامـي» (1986م)، يضـم مجموعـة مـن لوحاتـه مصحوبة بمجموعـة مـن المقـالات التي تسـلط الضـوء على فنه ورؤيته. أما معرضه الفـردي الثاني، الذي نظمته الجمعيـة العربية السـعودية للثقافة والفنون، فقد أقيم فـي أبها عـام 1988م.

شـارك خليـل فـي العديـد مـن المعـارض الجماعيـة، بـدءاً مـن معـرض الفـن السـعودي المعاصر بالرياض(1979م)، ثم معرض كبار الفنانين السـعوديين (1980م) بالرياض، و المعرض الجماعي الثانـي في صالة العرض العالمية الـذي نظمته دار الفنون السـعودية بالرياض (1981م)، بالإضافة إلى المعرض الافتتاحي لفرع الجمعية العربية السعودية للثقافـة والفنـون فـي جـازان (2002م).

وعلى الصعيد العالمي، شـارك خليل في الأسبوع الثقافـي لـدول مجلـس التعـاون الخليجـي بباريس، فرنسـا (1981م)، ومعـرض الفن السـعودي المعاصر في بـون، ألمانيـا (1981م)، ومعـرض الطاقة الدولي بنيويـورك، الولايـات المتحـدة الأمريكيـة (1981م)، والمعـرض السـابع للفنانين التشـكيليين العـرب في الكويت العاصمـة، الكويـت (1981م)، ومعرض الفن السعودي المعاصر، عمان، الأردن (1982م)، ومهرجان الشـباب العربي ببغداد، العراق (1982م)؛ والأسـبوع الثقافـي السـعودي بالمغـرب، والأسـبوع الثقافـي العربي بالسويد (1983م)، والمعرض الثامن للفنانين

He was part of the 3rd Cairo Biennale, Egypt (1988); the Second Festival of Fine Arts for the GCC, Doha, Qatar (1992); and the Contemporary Arab Plastic Arts pavilion in New Mexico, USA (1992). His work was recently featured in *Khamseen: 50 Years of Saudi Visual Arts*, Sotheby's, London, UK (2024).

Khaleel has received numerous accolades, including the first prize at the *Contemporary Saudi Art Exhibition* in Riyadh, Saudi Arabia (1979), and the first prize for *The Fifth General Exhibition for Formative Arts Collections* in Riyadh, Saudi Arabia (1981). In addition, for four consecutive years, he won first prize in the painting category in the exhibitions sponsored by the General Presidency of Youth Welfare (1981). He also received the Golden Sail Award, Kuwait City, Kuwait (1981); first prize at *The Seventh Exhibition for Formative Arts Collections*, Riyadh, Saudi Arabia (1983); first prize at *The Eighth Exhibition for Formative Arts Collections*, Riyadh, Saudi Arabia (1984); *Abha's Prize Exhibition*, Abha, Saudi Arabia (1989); and the Golden Palm Award, Riyadh, Saudi Arabia (1989).

A key figure in Saudi art history, Khaleel Hassan Khaleel has developed a distinctive style through his innovative concept of Dreamism: blending global and local influences, he pays homage to his native region. While deeply rooted in personal expression, his style maintains a universal resonance, transcending cultural boundaries through his visionary approach.

التشكيليين العرب في الكويت العاصمة، الكويت (1983م)، ومعرض الفنانين العالميين المعاصرين الثامن عشر في متحف موناكو الوطني بمونتي كارلو، موناكو (1984م)، وبينالي القاهرة الدولي الثالث، مصر (1988م)، ومهرجان الفن التشكيلي الثاني لدول مجلس التعاون الخليجي بالدوحة، قطر (1992م)، وجناح الفن التشكيلي العربي المعاصر في نيو مكسيكو بالولايات المتحدة الأمريكية (1992م). وعُرضت أعماله مؤخراً في معرض "خمسون عاماً من الفنون البصرية السعودية" في دار سوثبي للمزادات بلندن، المملكة المتحدة (2024م).

وقد حصل خلال مسيرته على العديد من الجوائز، ومن أبرزها الجائزة الأولى في معرض الفن السعودي المعاصر بالرياض، المملكة العربية السعودية (1979م)، والجائزة الأولى لمعرض المقتنيات الخامس بالرياض، المملكة العربية السعودية (1981م). بالإضافة إلى ذلك، حاز لأربع سنوات متتالية على الجائزة الأولى لفئة الرسم في المعارض التي رعتها الرئاسة العامة لرعاية الشباب (1981م). كما حصل على جائزة الشراع الذهبي بالمعرض السابع للفنانين التشكيليين العرب بالكويت (1981م)، والجائزة الأولى لمعرض المقتنيات السابع بالرياض، المملكة العربية السعودية (1983م)، والجائزة الأولى لمعرض المقتنيات الثامن بالرياض، المملكة العربية السعودية (1984م)؛ وجائزة المعرض التشكيلي لجائزة أبها، المملكة العربية السعودية (1989م)، وجائزة السعفة الذهبية بمهرجان الفن التشكيلي الأول لدول مجلس التعاون الخليجي بالرياض، المملكة العربية السعودية (1989م).

خليل حسن خليل شهابٌ فنيٍّ لم يُغادر الأُفق، وعَلمٌ بارزٌ في تاريخ الفن السعودي، له خيال فذٌّ قاده لابتكار مفهوم "الحُلمية"، جامعاً فيه بين التأثيرات العالمية والأصالة المحلية، ومستلهماً من تراث منطقته الغني، وعلى الرغم من تجذّره العميق في التعبير الشخصي، فإن أسلوبه يحتفظ ببُعد عالمي يتخطى الحدود الثقافية، بفضل رؤيته الفنية الثاقبة ونهجه الإبداعي المميّز.

التسلسل الزمني لسيرة الفنان
Artist Timeline

1958

وُلد خليل حسن خليل في جازان بالمملكة العربية السعودية

Khaleel Hassan Khaleel was born in Jizan, Saudi Arabia

دمج الفـن فـي المناهج الدراسـية لجميـع المسـتويات في المـدارس الحكوميـة فـي نظـام التعليـم العام فـي المملكة العربية السـعودية

Art was incorporated into the general education curriculum across Saudi Arabia

1964

درس خليـل المرحلـة الابتدائية بمدرسـة الملك سـعود في جـازان، المملكة العربية السـعودية

Khaleel attended King Saud Elementary School in Jizan, Saudi Arabia

1965

تأسـيس معهد التربية الفنية للمعلمين في الرياض بالمملكة العربية السعودية

The Institute of Art Education established its first location in Riyadh, Saudi Arabia

1973

تأسيس الجمعية العربية السعودية للثقافة والفنون بالرياض، وافتتاح ثلاثة عشـر فرعـاً لها في مختلف أنحـاء المملكة في الأعوام التالية

The Saudi Arabian Society for Culture and Arts was established in Riyadh, Saudi Arabia; in the following years, it opened thirteen branches across the Kingdom

1974

تأسـيس الرئاسـة العامة لرعاية الشـباب كمؤسسـة حكومية مسـتقلة، مع قسـم تابع لها للفنون التشـكيلية فـي الرياض بالمملكة العربية السـعودية

The General Presidency of Youth Welfare was established as an independent governmental institution with a dedicated Fine Arts Department in Riyadh, Saudi Arabia

1976

تخرّج خليل من معهد التربيـة الفنية في الرياض بالمملكة العربية السعودية

Khaleel graduated from the Institute of Art Education in Riyadh, Saudi Arabia

1977

أسس مرسمه الخاص في جازان، المملكة العربية السعودية

Khaleel established his private studio in Jizan, Saudi Arabia

1979

شارك في معرض الفن السعودي المعاصر بالرياض، المملكة العربية السعودية

Khaleel participated in *The Contemporary Saudi Art Exhibition* in Riyadh, Saudi Arabia

حصـل علـى الجائـزة الأولـى فـي معـرض الفن السـعودي المعاصر مـن الرئاسـة العامـة لرعايـة الشـباب

Khaleel received first prize at *The Contemporary Saudi Art Exhibition* from the General Presidency of Youth Welfare in Riyadh, Saudi Arabia

تأسـيس دار الفنـون السـعودية على يـد محمد السـليم في الرياض، المملكة العربية السعودية، والتي أضيفت إليها لاحقاً صالـة العـرض العالمية التي تسـتضيف الفنانـين الوطنيين والعالميين

The Saudi Art House was established in Riyadh, Saudi Arabia, by Mohammed Alsaleem; the International Gallery, which exhibits works by both national and international artists, was later added

1980

نال خليل الميدالية الذهبية من نادي الطائف الأدبي

Khaleel won the Golden Medal from the Taif Literary Club

شارك في معرض كبار الفنانين السعوديين بالرياض، المملكة العربية السعودية

Khaleel participated in the *Great Saudi Exhibition* in Riyadh, Saudi Arabia

1981

Khaleel participated in the second group exhibition at the International Gallery, organized by the Saudi Art House in Riyadh, Saudi Arabia

Khaleel participated in *The Cultural Week of the Gulf Cooperation Council Countries* in Paris, France

Khaleel participated in *The Contemporary Saudi Art Exhibition* in Bonn, Germany

Khaleel was selected by the Ministry of Commerce to exhibit in the Saudi pavilion at the *International Exhibition for Energy* in New York, USA

Khaleel received the first prize for *The Fifth General Exhibition for Formative Arts Collections* in Riyadh, Saudi Arabia

Khaleel won first prize for four consecutive years beginning this year in the painting category of the Formative Arts Collection exhibitions by the General Presidency of Youth Welfare, Riyadh, Saudi Arabia

Khaleel participated in the *Seventh Kuwait Exhibition for Arab Artists* in Kuwait City, Kuwait, organized by the Kuwait Society for Formative Arts, where he received the Golden Sail Award, a merit prize

شــارك فـي المعـرض الجماعـي الثانـي فـي صالة العـرض العالمية الذي نظمته دار الفنون السعودية بالرياض، المملكة العربية السعودية

شــارك في الاسـبوع الثقافي لدول مجلس التعاون الخليجي بباريس، فرنسا

شارك في معرض الفن السعودي المعاصر في بون، ألمانيا

اختيــر مـن قبل وزارة التجـارة لعـرض أعمالـه فـي الجنـاح السـعودي في معـرض الطاقة الدولي بنيويورك، الولايات المتحـدة الأمريكية

حصل على الجائـزة الأولى بمعرض المقتنيـات الخامس في الرياض، المملكة العربية السعودية

حصـل علـى الجائـزة الأولى لأربـع سـنوات متتالية فـي فئة الرسـم بمعـارض المقتنيـات التـي أقامتهـا الرئاسـة العامـة لرعاية الشباب

شــارك فـــي المعـرض السابع للفنانين التشكيليين العرب في الكويـت العاصمـة، الكويـت، الذي نظمته جمعية الكويتية للفنـون التشكيلية، وحصـل علــى جائـزة الشـراع الذهبـي

1982

Khaleel participated in *The Contemporary Saudi Art Exhibition* in Amman, Jordan, organized by the General Presidency of Youth Welfare

Khaleel participated in the *Arab Youth Festival* in Baghdad, Iraq

Khaleel participated in the biennial exhibition in Morocco organized by the General Presidency of Youth Welfare

شارك في معرض الفن السعودي المعاصر في عمّان بالأردن

شارك في مهرجان الشباب العربي في بغداد، العراق

شـارك في معرض السنتين في المغرب الذي نظمته الرئاسة العامة لرعاية الشباب

1983

Khaleel participated in *The Eighth Kuwait Exhibition for Arab Artists* in Kuwait City, Kuwait

Khaleel participated in the *Saudi Art Cultural Week* in Morocco, organized by the General Presidency of Youth Welfare

Khaleel received first prize at the *Seventh Exhibition for Formative Arts Collections* in Riyadh, Saudi Arabia

Khaleel participated in the *Arab Cultural Week* in Sweden, organized by the General Presidency of Youth Welfare

شـارك في المعـرض الثامـن للفنانين التشـكيليين العرب في الكويت العاصمـة، الكويت

شارك في الأسبوع الثقافي السعودي بالمغرب، الذي نظمته الرئاسة العامة لرعاية الشباب

حصـل علـى الجائـزة الأولـى بمعرض المقتنيـات السـابع بالريـاض، المملكـة العربيـة السـعودية

شــارك في الأسـبوع الثقافي العربي بالسـويد، الـذي نظمته الرئاسـة العامة لرعاية الشـباب

1984

Khaleel participated in the eighteenth *International Prize for Contemporary Art* exhibition, organized by the Prince Pierre Foundation at the National Museum of Monaco in Monte Carlo, Monaco

Khaleel participated in the *Saudi Contemporary Exhibition* in New Delhi, India, organized by the General Presidency of Youth Welfare

Khaleel received first prize at *The Eighth Exhibition for Formative Arts Collections* in Riyadh, Saudi Arabia

شــارك فـي معـرض الفنانيـن العالميين المعاصريـن الثامن عشـر، الذي نظمته مؤسسـة الأمير بيير في متحـف موناكو الوطنـي بمونتي كارلـو، موناكو

شارك في معرض الفن السعودي المعاصر فـي نيودلهي بالهند، الـذي نظمته الرئاسة العامة لرعاية الشباب

حصل على الجائزة الأولى بمعرض المقتنيات الثامن بالرياض، المملكة العربية السعودية

Khaleel participated in the *Ninth Kuwait Exhibition for Arab Artists* in Kuwait City, Kuwait Khaleel participated in the nineteenth *International Prize for Contemporary Art* exhibition, organized by the Prince Pierre Foundation at the National Museum of Monaco in Monte Carlo, Monaco	**1985**	شـارك فـي المعـرض التاسـع للفنانيـن التشكيليين العـرب في الكويت العاصمة، الكويت شارك في معرض الفنانيـن العالمييـن المعاصرين التاسـع عشـر، الذي نظمته مؤسسة الأمير بيير في متحـف موناكو الوطنـي بمونتي كارلـو، موناكو
Khaleel held his first solo exhibition, organized by the Jizan Literary Club in Jizan, Saudi Arabia The Jizan Literary Club published a book of Khaleel's works with accompanying essays titled *My Dreams* Khaleel participated in the second edition of *Alwadi*, an exhibition held by the Jizan Literary Club in Jizan, Saudi Arabia	**1986**	معرضـه الفردي الأول بتنظيم نادي جـازان الأدبي بجازان، المملكـة العربية السعودية أصدر له نادي جـازان الأدبـي كتابـاً بعنوان «أحلامـي» يضم لوحاتـه مصحوبـة بمجموعة مـن المقالات شـارك فـي النسـخة الثانية لمعـرض الـوادي بتنظيـم نادي جـازان الأدبـي بجازان، المملكـة العربية السعودية
Khaleel participated in the 3rd Cairo Biennale in Cairo, Egypt Khaleel held his second solo exhibition, organized by the Saudi Arabian Society for Culture and Arts, in Abha, Saudi Arabia	**1988**	شـارك في بينالي القاهرة الدولي الثالث بمصر معرضـه الفردي الثانـي بتنظيم الجمعية العربية السعودية للثقافة والفنـون، بأبها، المملكـة العربية السـعودية
Khaleel received *Abha's Prize Exhibition* in Abha, Saudi Arabia Khaleel received the Golden Palm Award at the first Plastic Arts Festival for the Gulf Cooperation Council (GCC) in Riyadh, Saudi Arabia The Al Muftaha Arts Village was founded in Abha, Saudi Arabia, by the Governor of Asir, Prince Khalid bin Faisal Al Saud; at the opening ceremony, Khaleel participated in the group exhibition with two artworks	**1989**	شـارك في المعـرض التشـكيلي لجائـزة أبها، المملكـة العربية السعودية حاز علـى جائزة السـعفة الذهبيـة بمهرجان الفن التشكيلي الأول لـدول مجلـس التعـاون الخليجـي بالريـاض، المملكـة العربية السـعودية تأسـيس قرية المفتاحة فـي أبها على يد أمير منطقة عسـير صاحـب السـمو الملكـي الأميـر خالد بـن فيصل آل سـعود، ومشـاركة خليل بلوحتيـن في المعـرض الافتتاحي
Khaleel participated in the Second Festival of Fine Arts for the GCC in Doha, Qatar Khaleel participated in the Contemporary Arab Plastic Arts pavilion in New Mexico, USA	**1992**	شـارك فـي مهرجـان الفن التشـكيلي الثانـي لـدول مجلس التعـاون الخليجـي بالدوحـة، قطر شـارك فـي جنـاح الفـن التشـكيلي العربـي المعاصر فـي نيو مكسـيكو بالولايـات الأمريكيـة المتحدة
The Saudi Arabian Society for Culture and Arts opened a branch in Jizan, Saudi Arabia; Khaleel participated in the inaugural exhibition in 2002	**2001**	افتتـاح فـرع الجمعية العربية السعودية للثقافـة والفنون في جـازان بالمملكـة العربية السعودية ومشـاركة خليل في المعـرض الافتتاحي فـي عـام 2002
Khaleel received a prize honoring teachers from the Ministry of Education at Ibn Sina Intermediate School in Jizan, Saudi Arabia	**2008**	حصـل علـى جائـزة وزارة التعليـم لتكريـم المعلميـن فـي متوسـطة ابـن سـينا بجـازان، المملكة العربية السـعودية
Misk Art Institute was established in Riyadh, Saudi Arabia	**2017**	تأسـيس معهـد مسـك للفنـون بالريـاض، المملكـة العربيـة السـعودية

Khaleel was honored by Misk Art Institute as a pioneer in Saudi arts	**2018**	تكريمه من قبل معهد مسك للفنون باعتباره من كبار رواد الفن السعودي
Khaleel was awarded an honorary prize by the Saudi Arabian Society for Culture and Arts in Jizan, Saudi Arabia	**2019**	حصل على جائزة فخرية من الجمعية العربية السعودية للثقافة والفنون بجازان، المملكة العربية السعودية
Khaleel was featured in the group exhibition *Khamseen: 50 Years of Saudi Visual Arts* at Sotheby's, London, United Kingdom	**2024**	شارك في المعرض الجماعي خمسون عاماً من الفنون البصرية السعودية في دار سوثبي للمزادات بلندن، المملكة المتحدة

الأعمال الفنية

Artworks

Self-portrait, 1977

Oil on canvas
93 × 80 cm
Courtesy of the artist

صورة الفنان، 1977

ألوان زيتية على قماش
93 × 80 سم
بإذن من الفنان

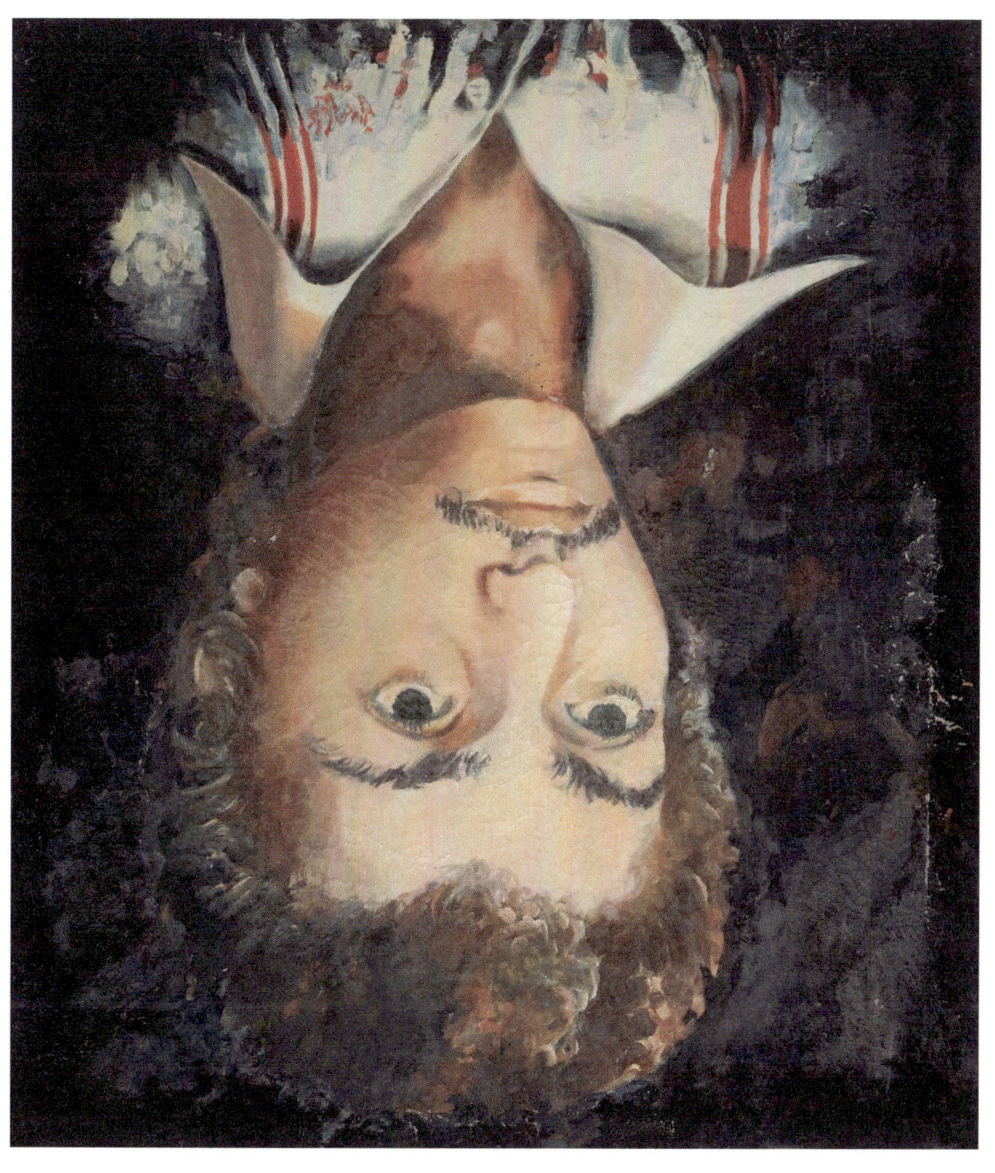

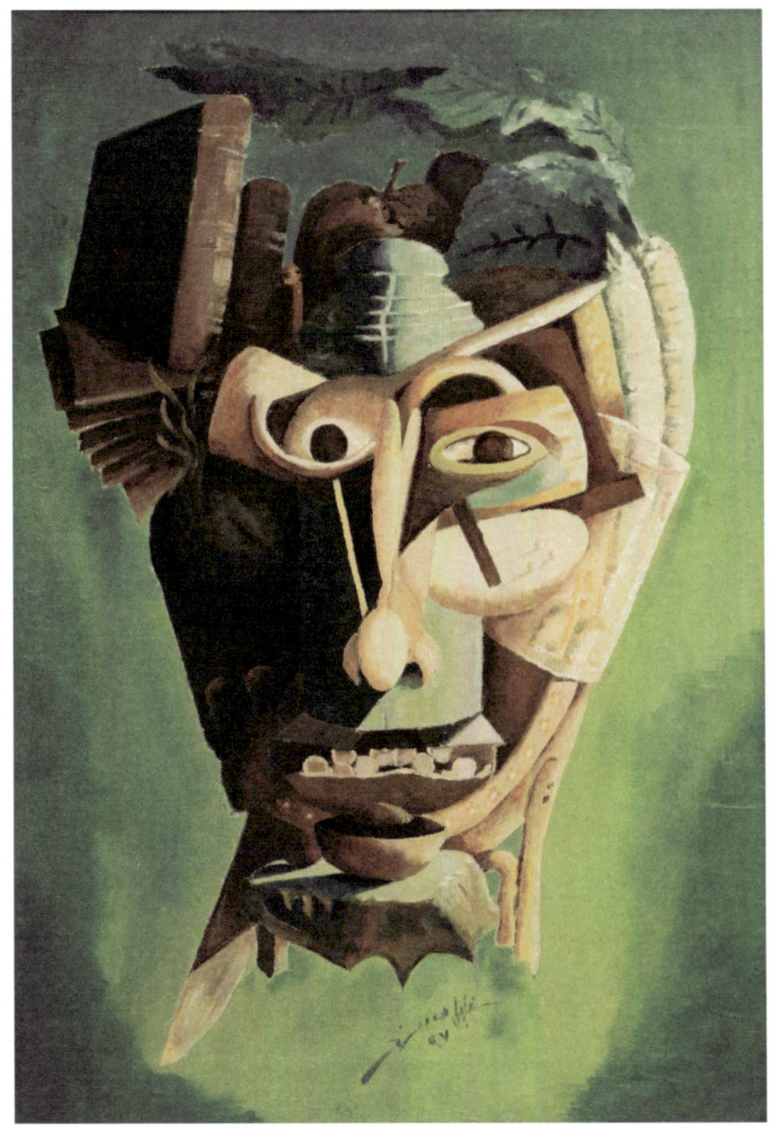

وجه، 1977

ألوان زيتية على قماش
67 × 46 سم
مجموعة محمد العلياني الخاصة، الرياض

Face, 1977

Oil on canvas
67 × 46 cm
Private collection of Mohammed Alalyani, Riyadh

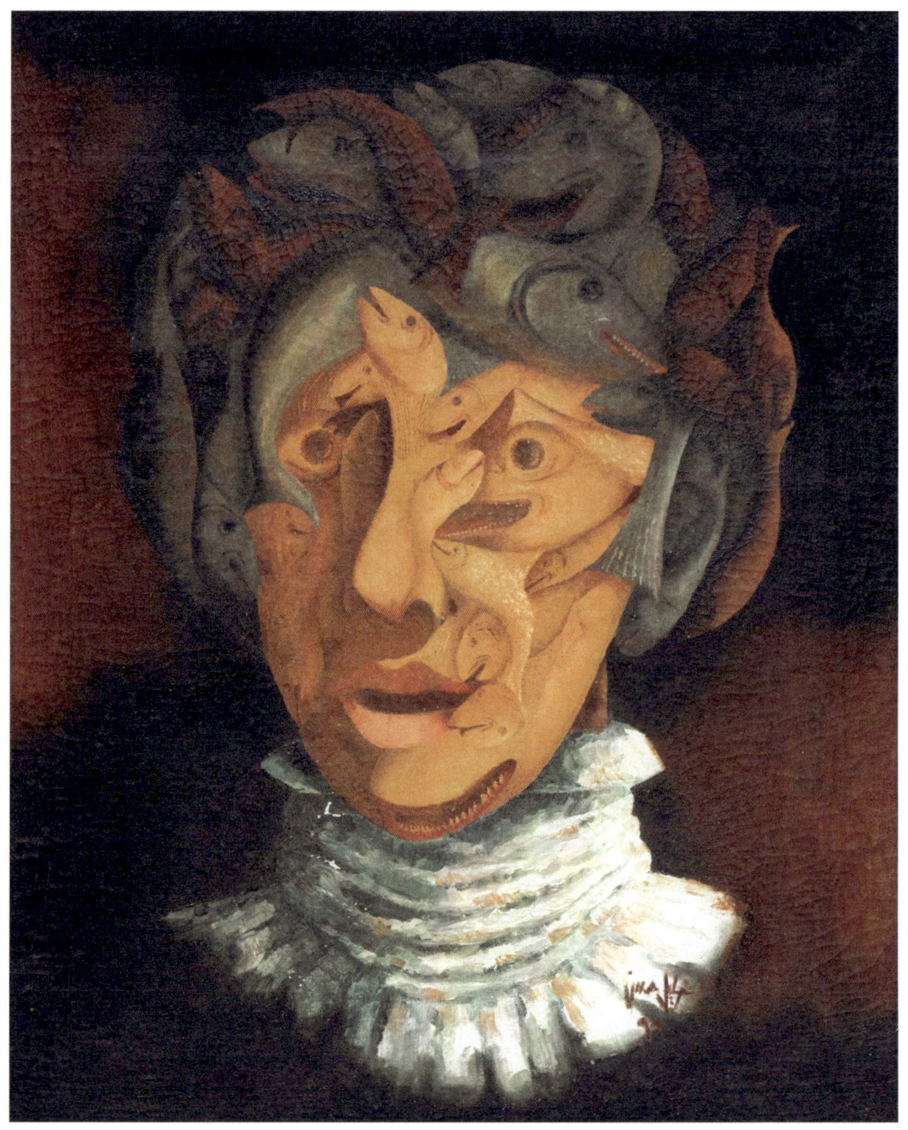

Face (2), 1978

Oil on canvas
61 × 50 cm
Private collection of Mohammed Alalyani, Riyadh

وجه *(2)*، 1978

ألوان زيتية على قماش
61 × 50 سم
مجموعة محمد العلياني الخاصة، الرياض

الإنسان والآلة، 1977

ألوان زيتية على قماش
97 × 76 سم
مجموعة محمد العلياني الخاصة، الرياض

Human and Machine, 1977

Oil on canvas
97 × 76 cm
Private collection of Mohammed Alalyani, Riyadh

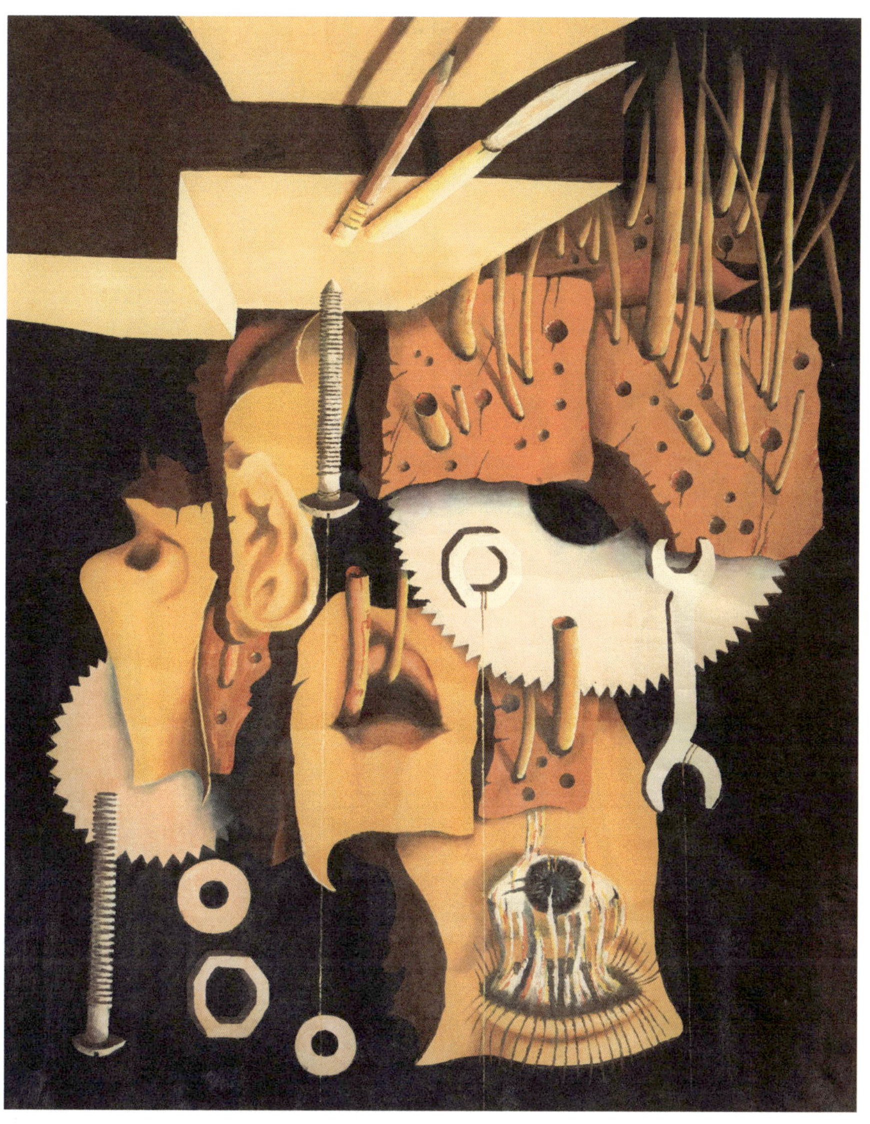

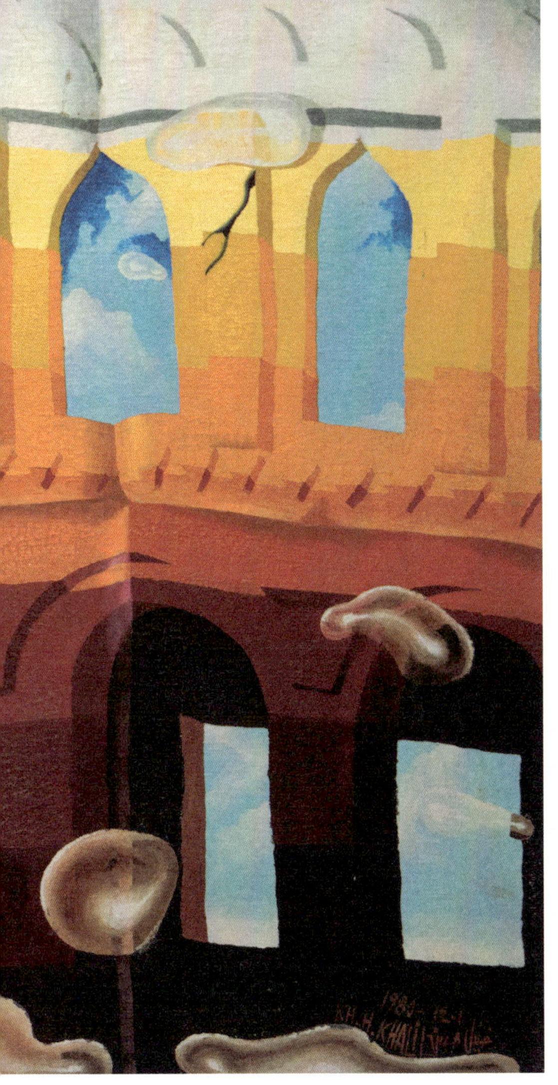

قطرات الندى، 1981

ألوان زيتية على قماش
55 × 85 سم
بإذن من الفنان

Dewdrop, 1981

Oil on canvas
55 × 85 cm
Courtesy of the artist

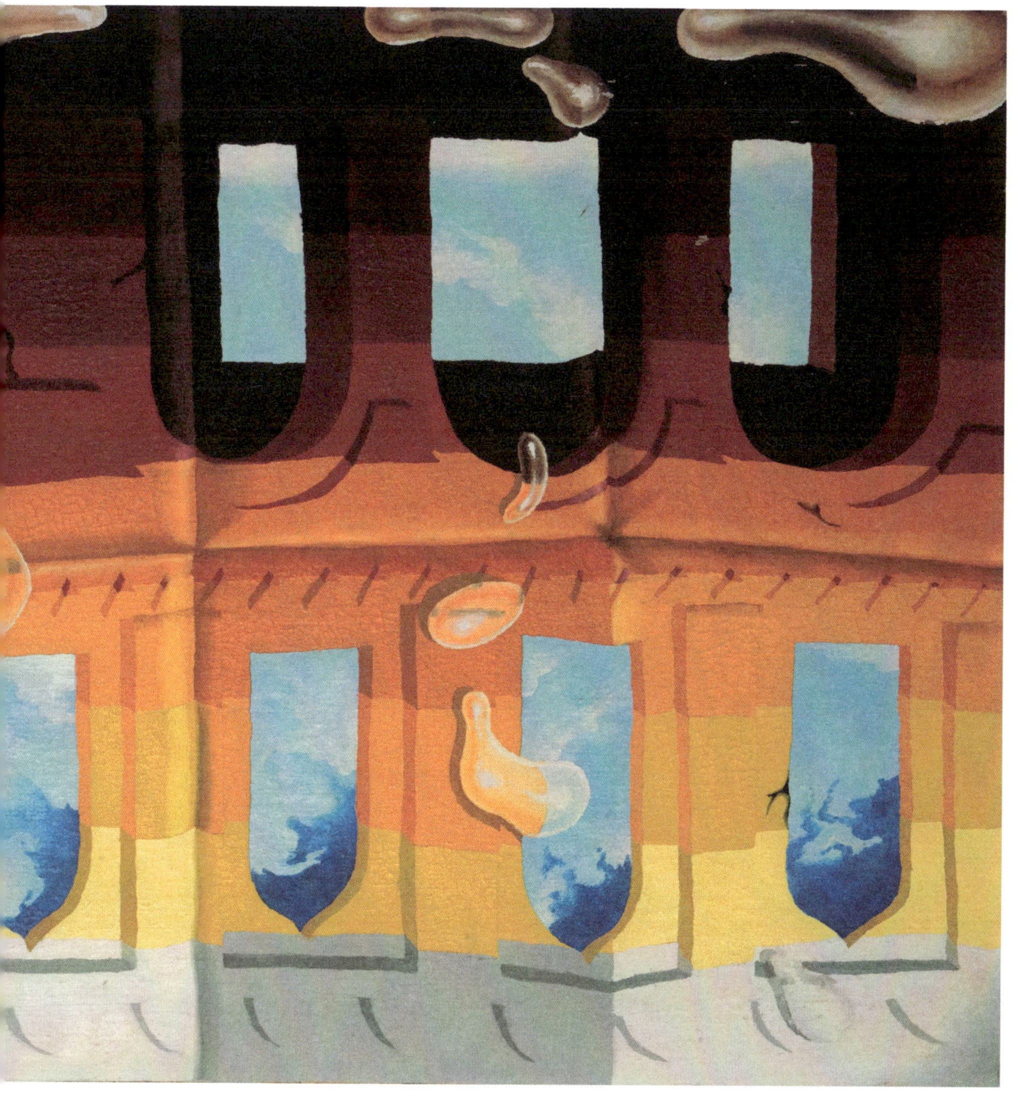

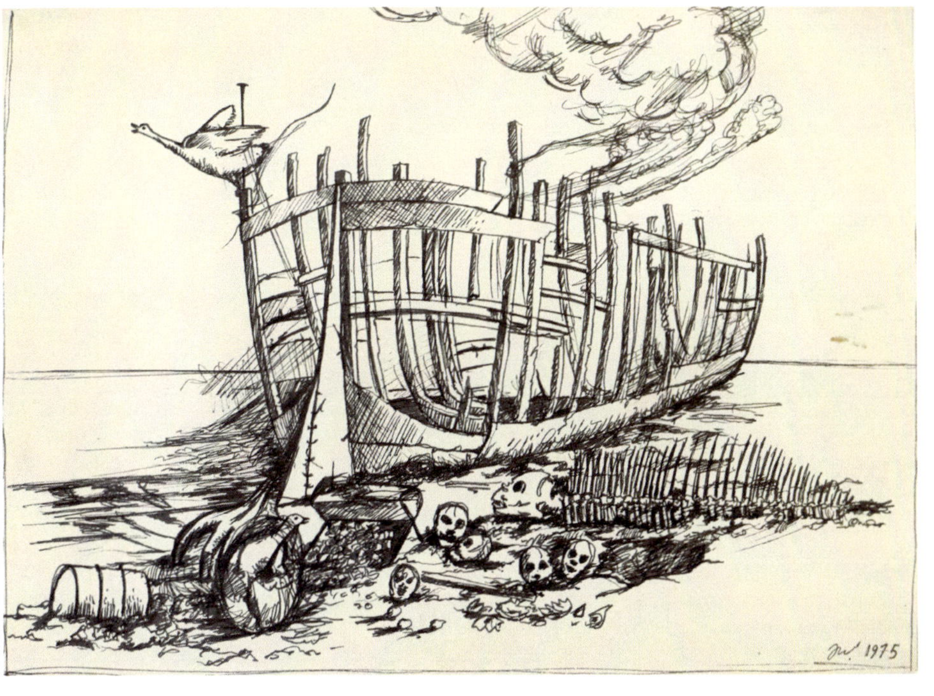

The End,
preparatory drawing, 1975

Ink on paper
22.5 × 31 cm
Courtesy of the artist

رسمة تحضيرية
لعمل النهاية، 1977

حبر على ورق
22.5 × 31 سم
بإذن من الفنان

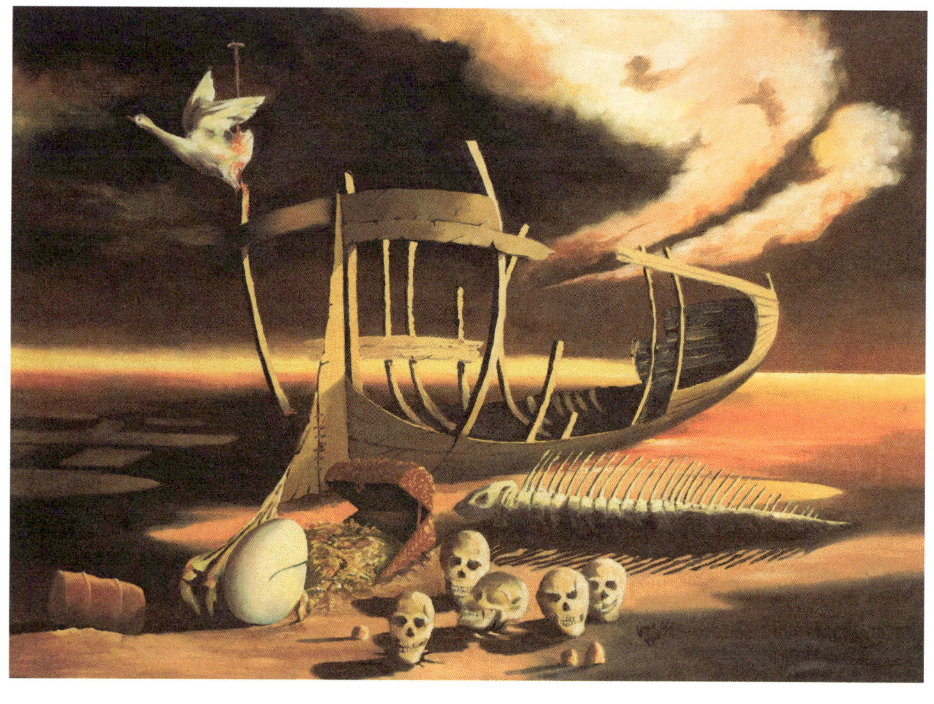

The End, 1977

Oil on canvas
66 × 90 cm
Private collection of Mohammed Alalyani, Riyadh

النهاية، 1977

ألوان زيتية على قماش
66 × 90 سم
مجموعة محمد العلياني الخاصة، الرياض

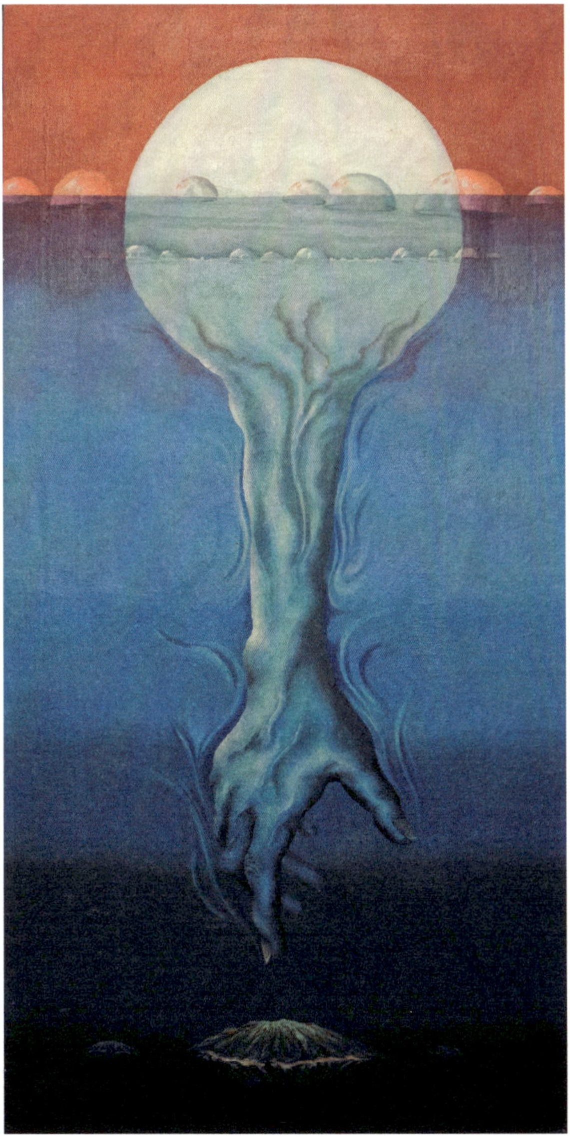

الغوص، 1981

ألوان زيتية على قماش
44 × 88 سم
بإذن من الفنان

Diving, 1981

Oil on canvas
88 × 44 cm
Courtesy of the artist

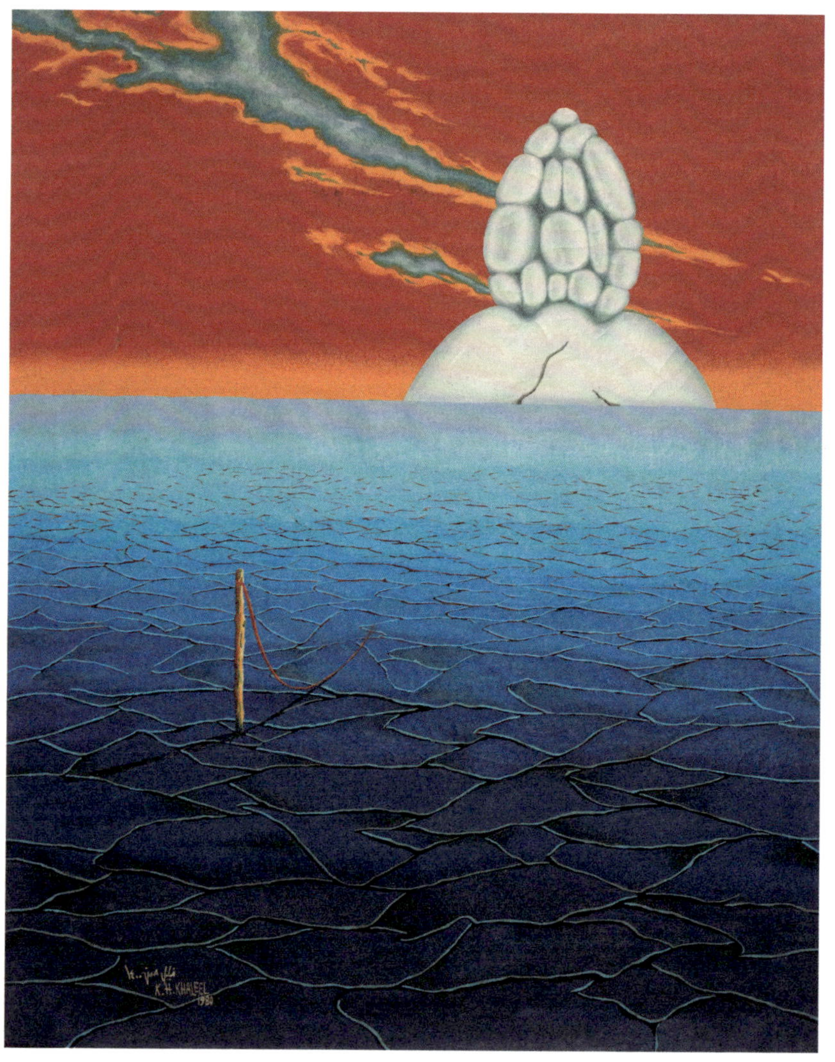

Summer Night Dream, 1980

Oil on canvas
96 × 76 cm
Courtesy of the artist

حلم ليلة صيف، 1980

ألوان زيتية على قماش
96 × 76 سم
بإذن من الفنان

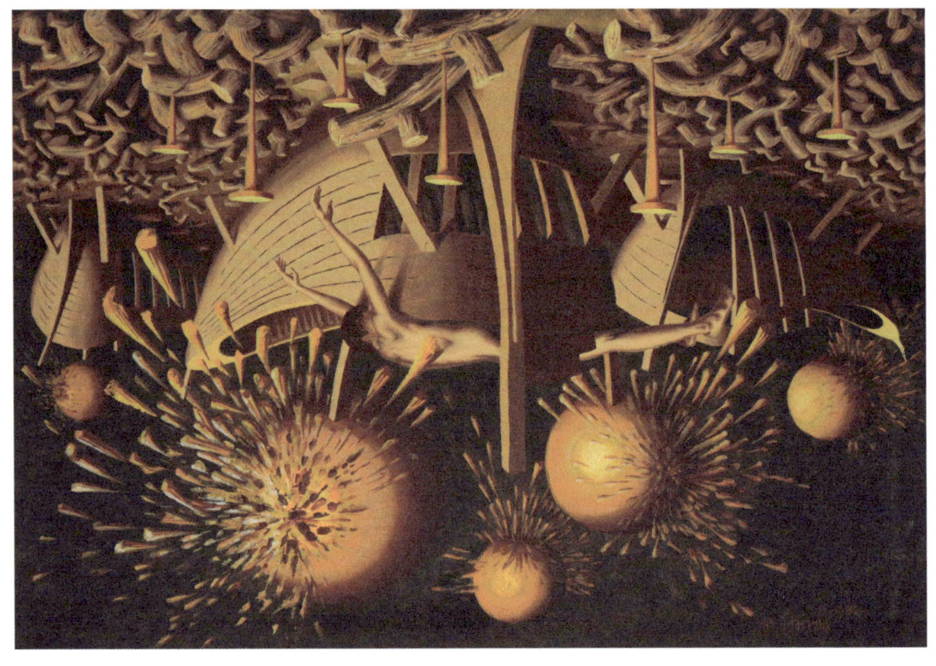

Ships Manufacturing, 1988

Oil on canvas
76 × 106 cm
Courtesy of the artist

صناعة السفن، 1988

ألوان زيتية على قماش
76 × 106 سم
بإذن من الفنان

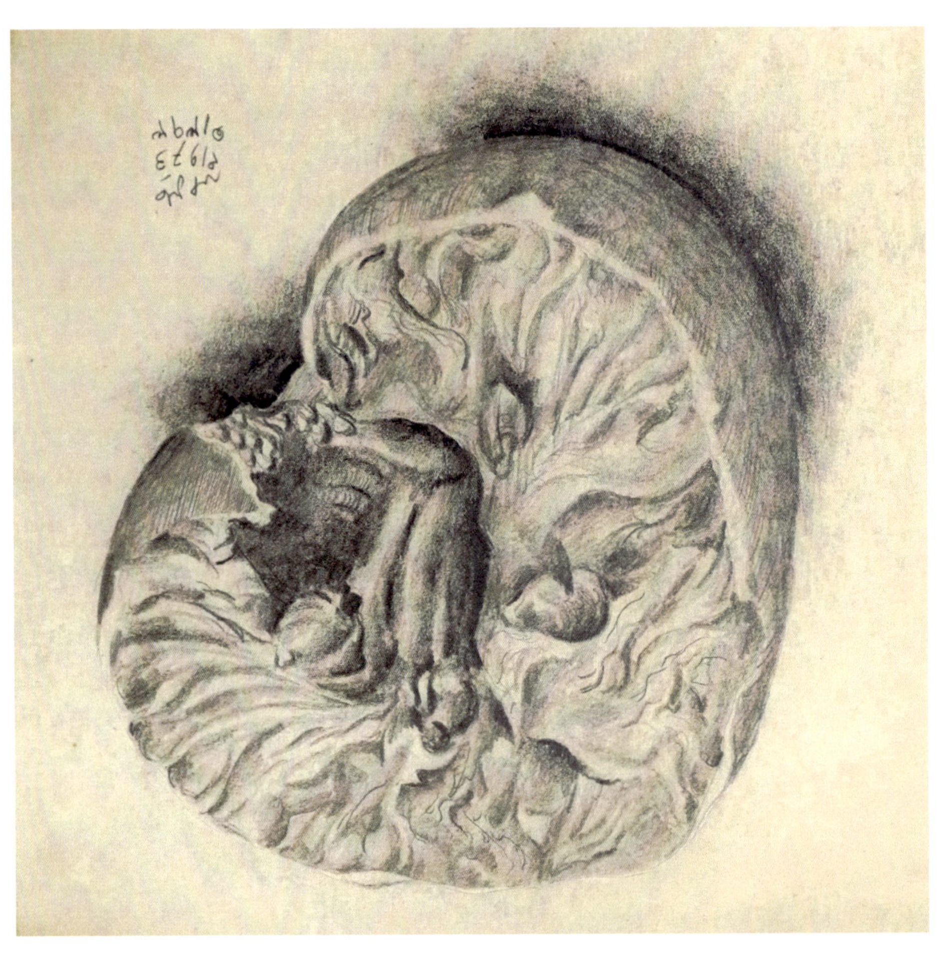

دراسة لبرتقالة، 1973

قلم رصاص على ورق
22 × 22.5 سم
بإذن من الفنان

Study of an Orange, 1973

Graphite on paper
22 × 22.5 cm
Courtesy of the artist

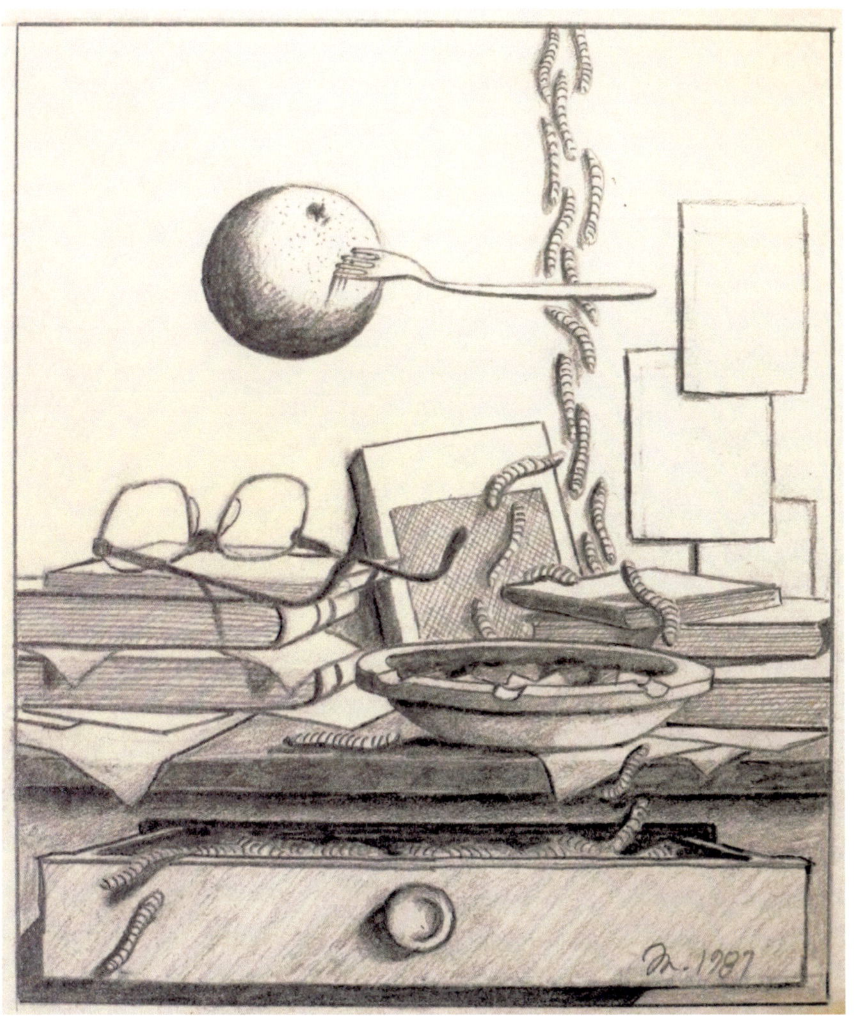

رسمة تحضيرية
لعمل *الدود،* 1987

قلم رصاص على ورق
20.5 × 17 سم
بإذن من الفنان

Worm,
preparatory drawing, 1987

Graphite on paper
20.5 × 17 cm
Courtesy of the artist

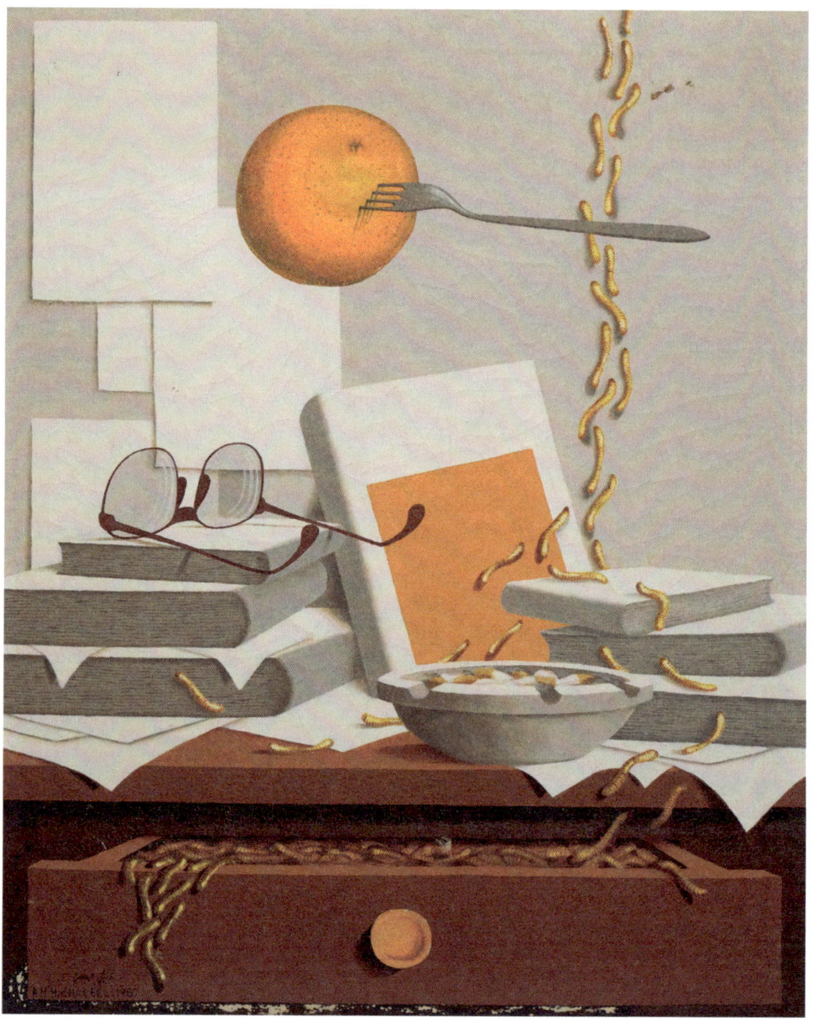

الدود، 1987

ألوان زيتية على قماش
80 × 65 سم
بإذن من الفنان

Worm, 1987

Oil on canvas
80 × 65 cm
Courtesy of the artist

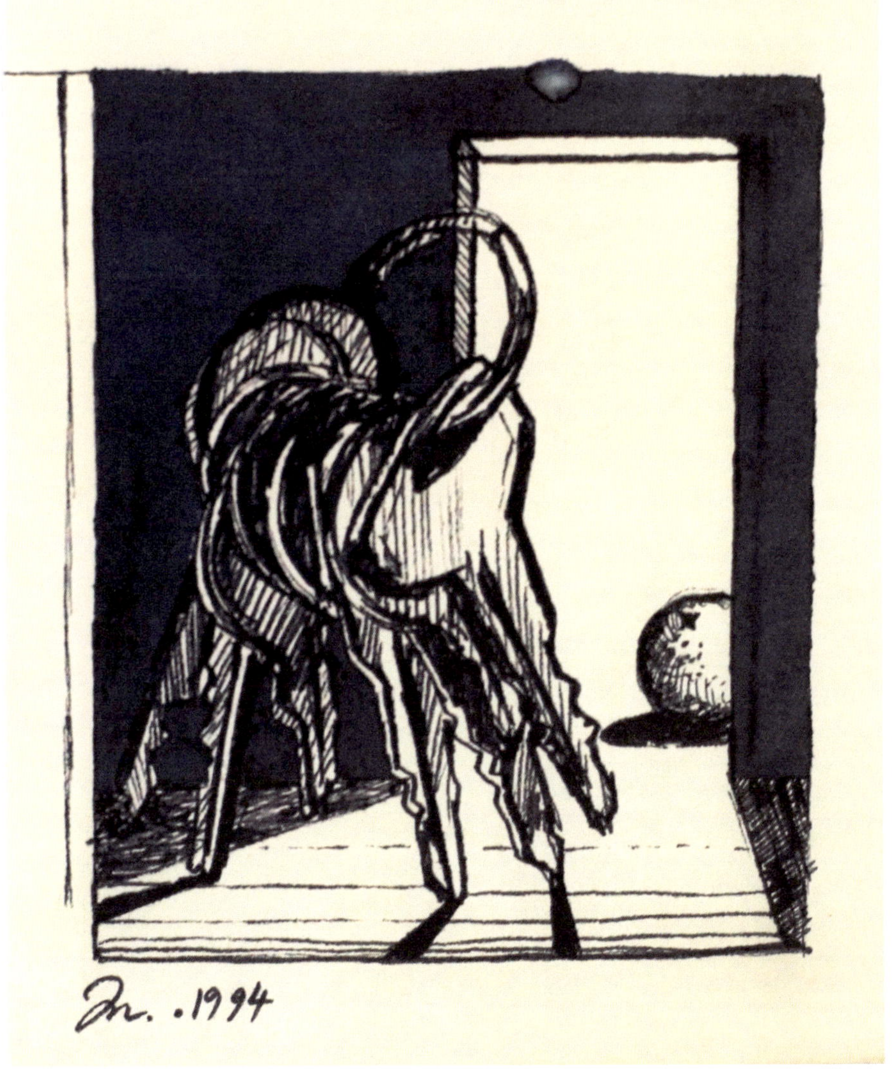

دراسة تحضيرية لعمل *مفاتح،* 1994

حبر على ورق
11.5 × 9.5 سم
بإذن من الفنان

Keys, preparatory study, 1994

Ink on paper
11.5 × 9.5 cm
Courtesy of the artist

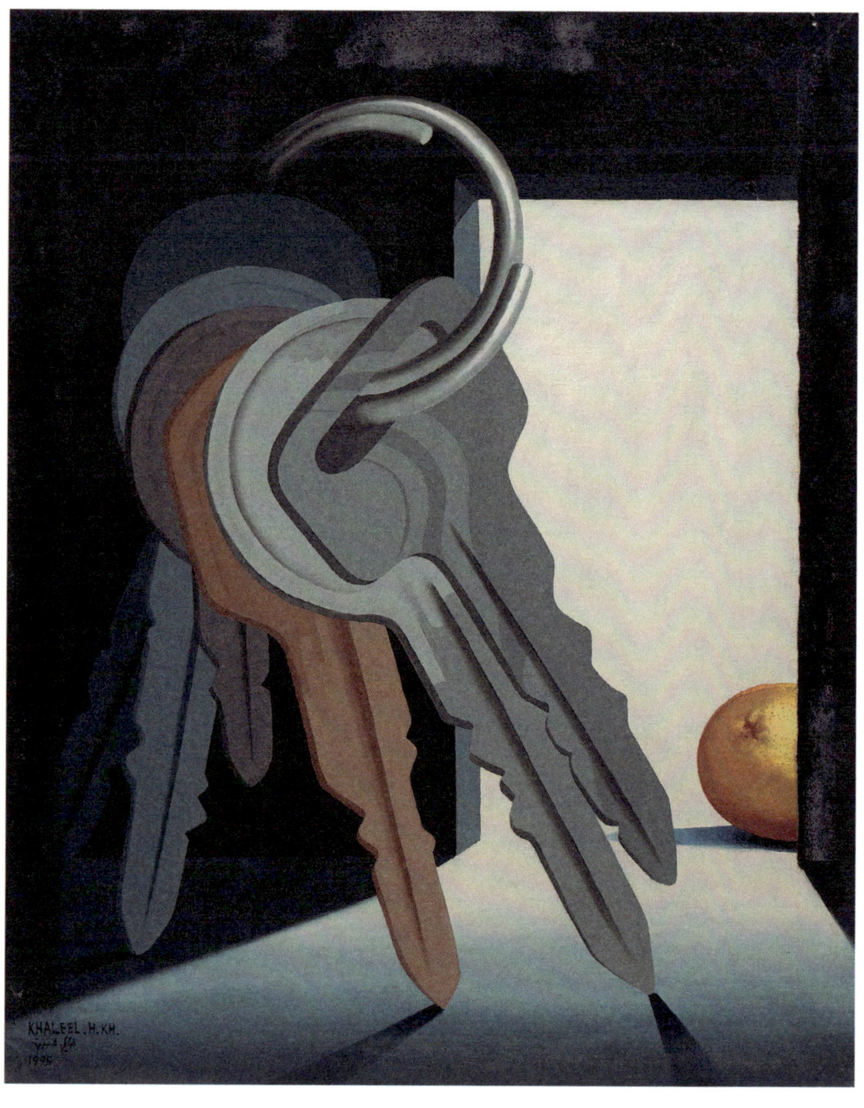

مفاتح، 1995

ألوان زيتية على قماش
86 × 68 سم
بإذن من الفنان

Keys, 1995

Oil on canvas
86 × 68 cm
Courtesy of the artist

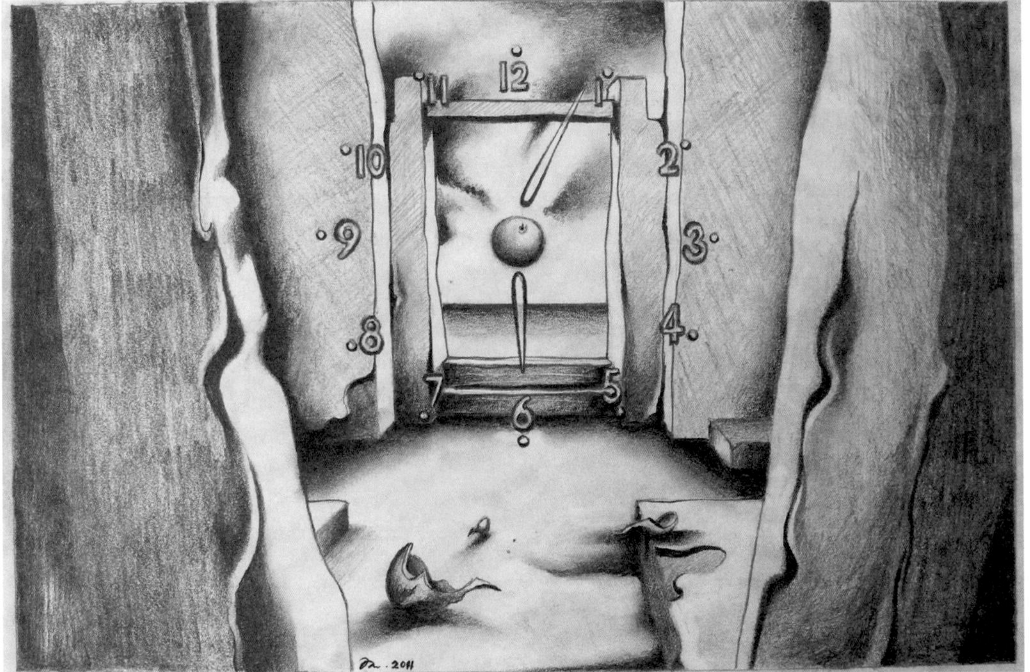

Sulaymaniyah Time,
preparatory drawing, 2011

Graphite on paper
22 × 32 cm
Courtesy of the artist

رسمة تحضيرية
لعمل الساعة السليمانية، 2011

قلم رصاص على ورق
22 × 32 سم
بإذن من الفنان

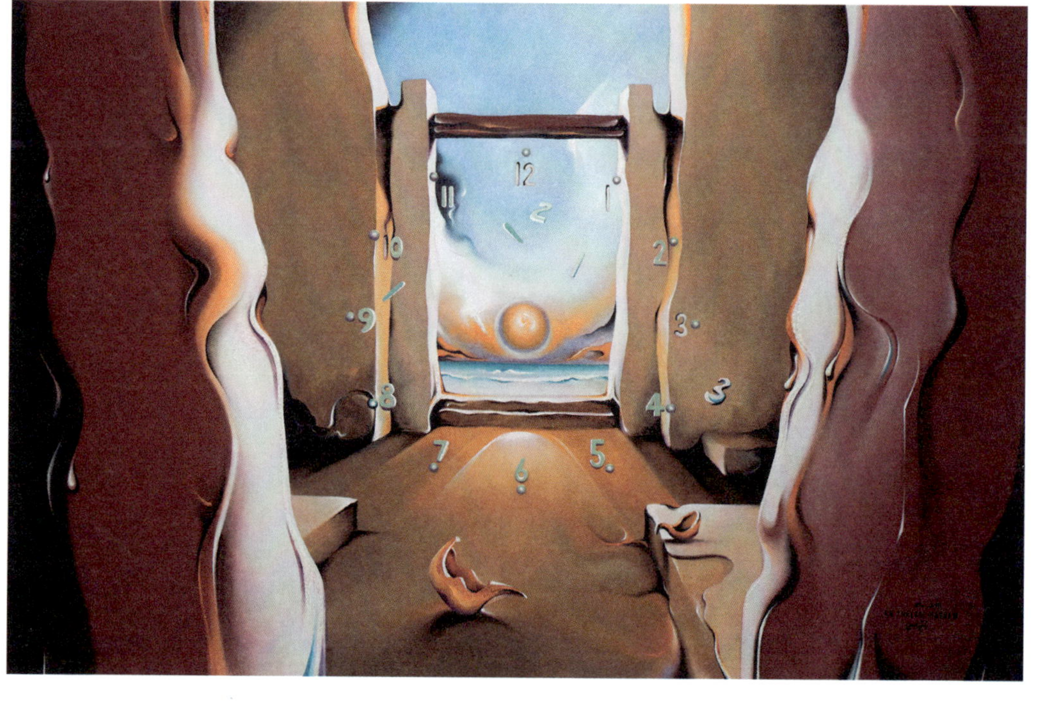

الساعة السليمانية، 2011

ألوان زيتية على قماش
100 × 150 سم
بإذن من الفنان

Sulaymaniyah Time, 2011

Oil on canvas
100 × 150 cm
Courtesy of the artist

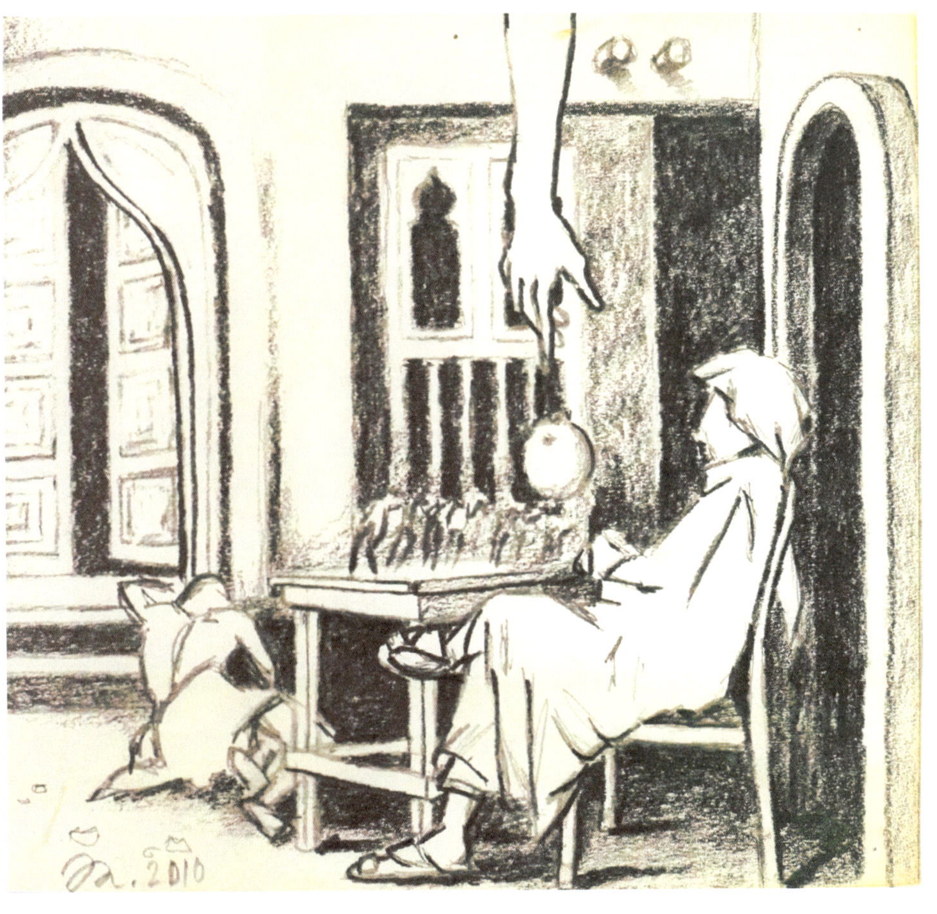

دراسة تحضيرية
لعمل قال الراوي، 2010

ألوان زيتية على قماش
19.5 × 21.5 سم
مجموعة خاصة

Al-rawi Said,
preparatory study, 2010

Graphite on paper
21.5 × 19.5 cm
Courtesy of the artist

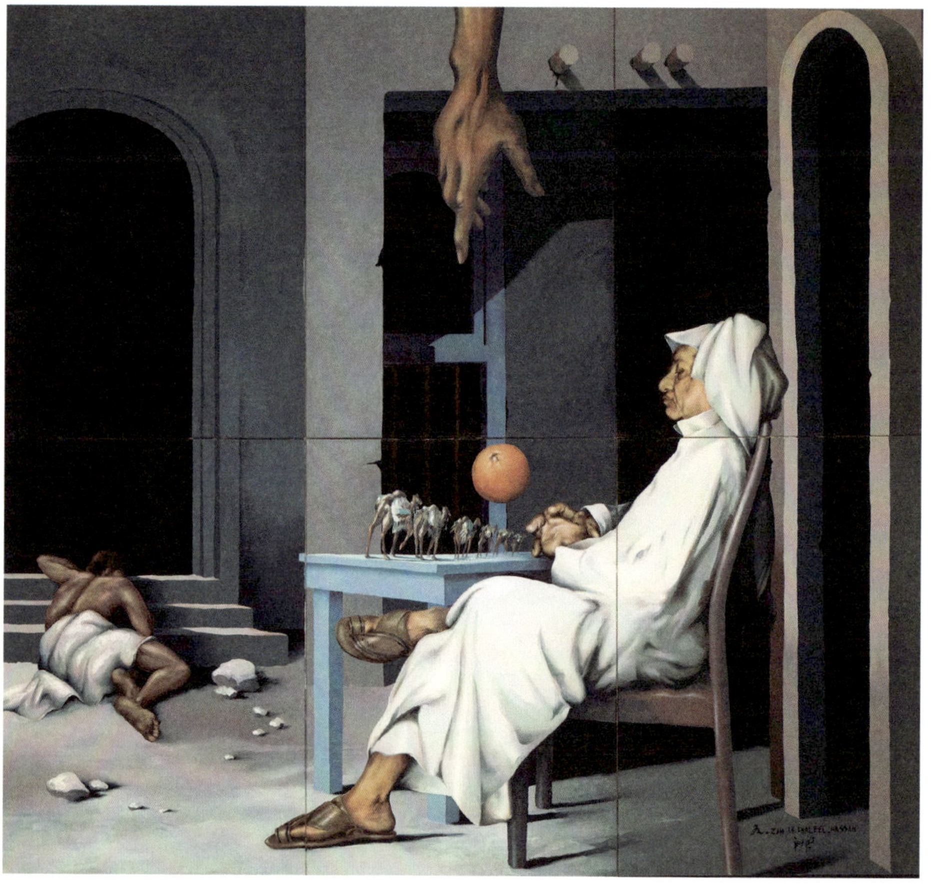

قال الراوي، 2010

ألوان زيتية على قماش
210 × 200 سم
مجموعة محمد العلياني الخاصة، الرياض

Al-rawi Said, 2010

Oil on canvas
210 × 200 cm
Private collection of Mohammed Alalyani, Riyadh

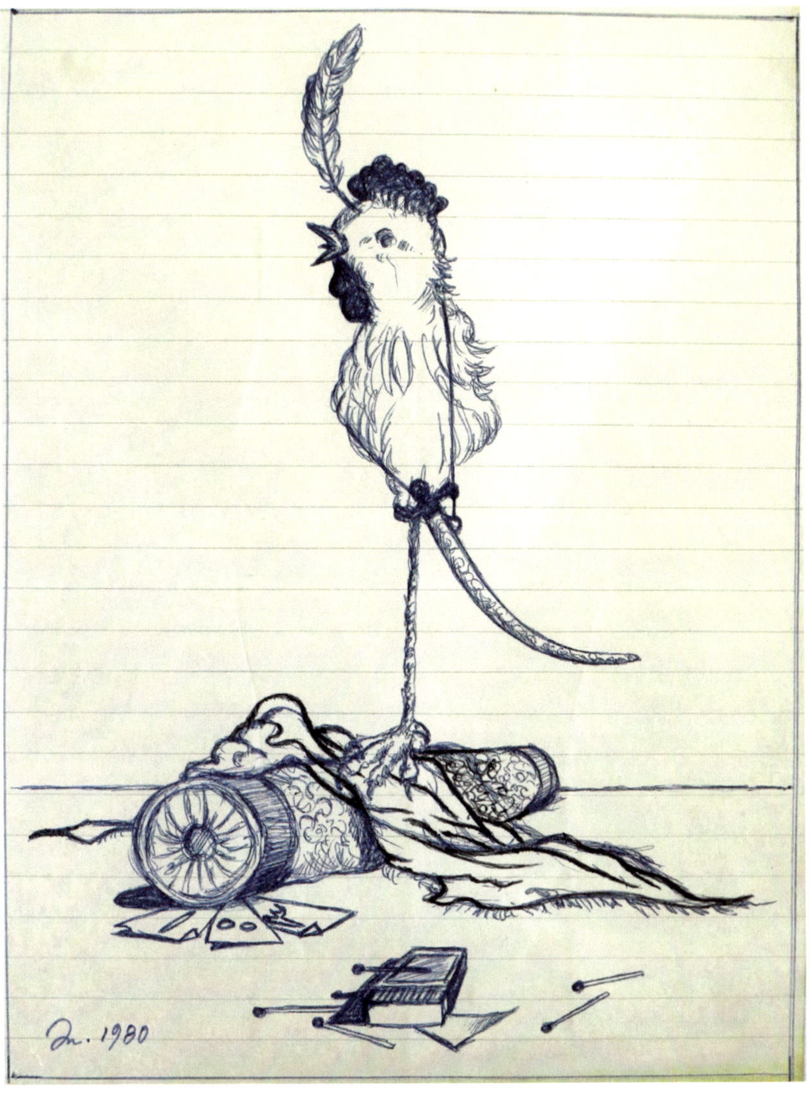

The Third Night After Thousand,
preparatory study, 1980

Ink on paper
21 × 15.5 cm
Courtesy of the artist

دراسة تحضيرية
لعمل الليلة الثالثة بعد الألف، 1980

حبر على ورق
15.5 × 21 سم
بإذن من الفنان

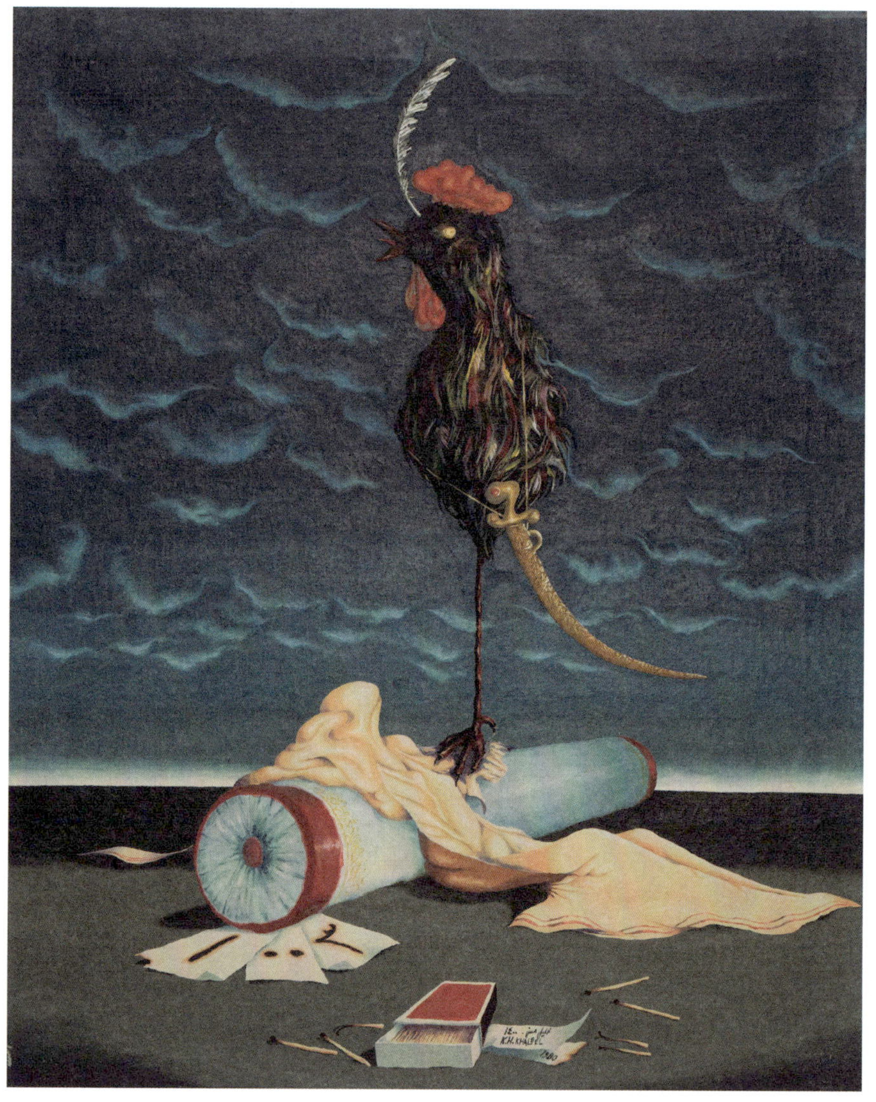

الليلة الثالثة بعد الألف،
1980

ألوان زيتية على قماش
96 × 75 سم
بإذن من الفنان

The Third Night After Thousand,
1980

Oil on canvas
96 × 75 cm
Courtesy of the artist

رسمة تحضيرية
لعمل لبنان (82)، 1982

قلم رصاص على ورق
21 × 14 سم
يإذن من الفنان

Lebanon (82),
preparatory drawing, 1982

Graphite on paper
21 × 14 cm
Courtesy of the artist

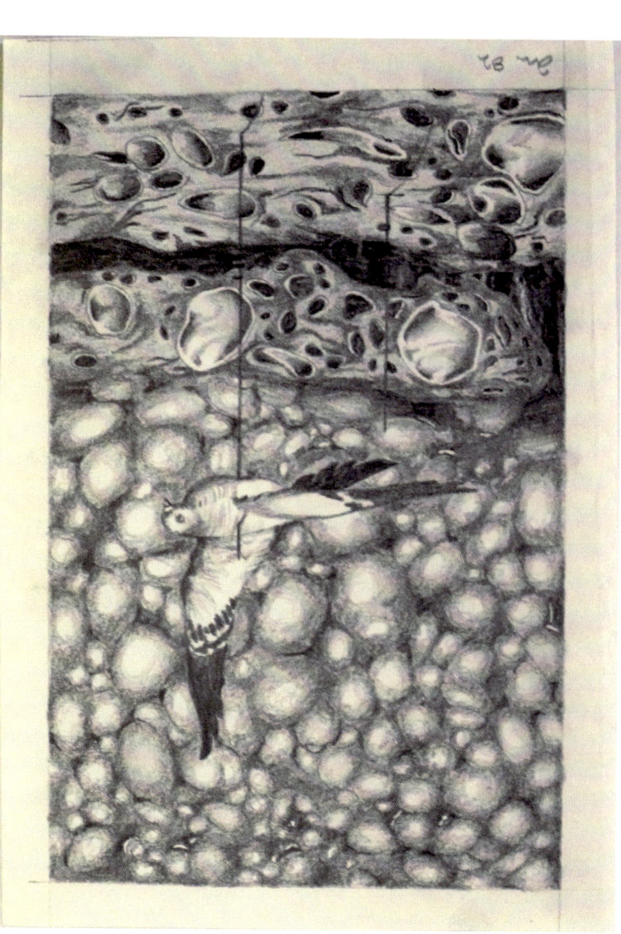

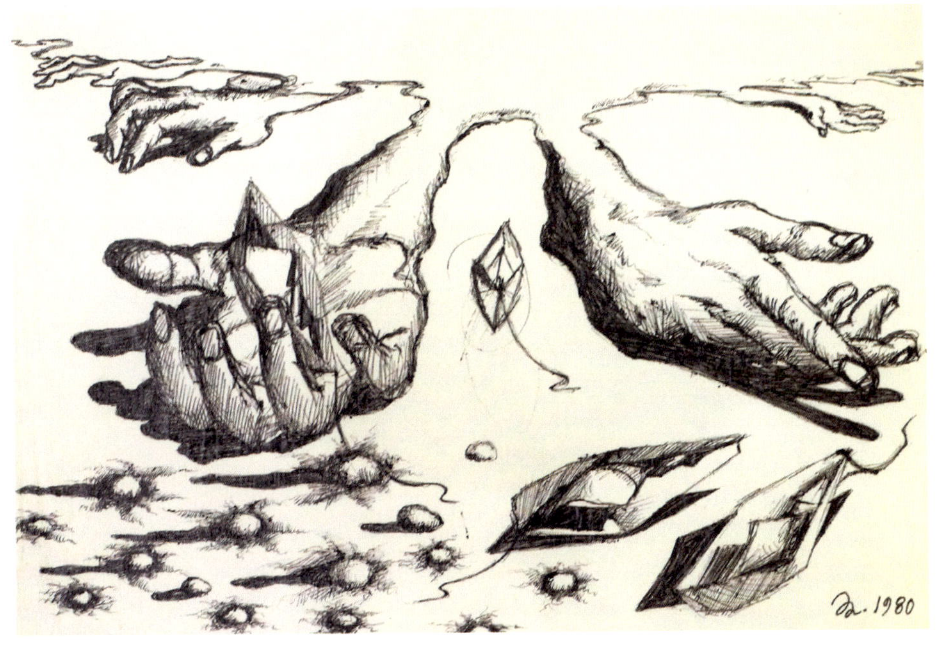

دراسة تحضيرية
لعمل *البحر،* 1980

حبر على ورق
16 × 24 سم
بإذن من الفنان

The Sea,
preparatory study, 1980

Ink on paper
16 × 24 cm
Courtesy of the artist

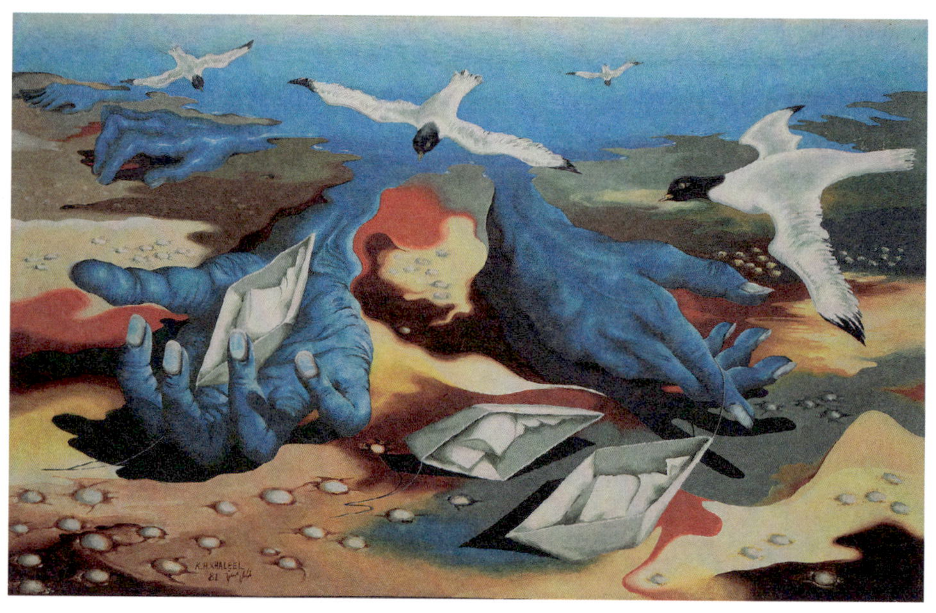

البحر، 1981

ألوان زيتية على قماش
64 × 100 سم
بإذن من الفنان

The Sea, 1981

Oil on canvas
64 × 100 cm
Courtesy of the artist

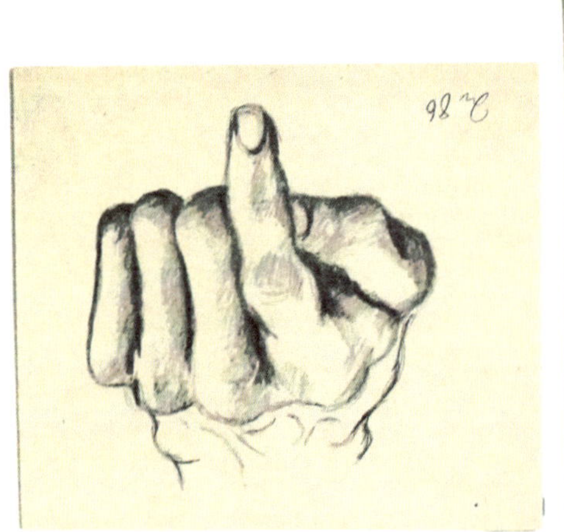

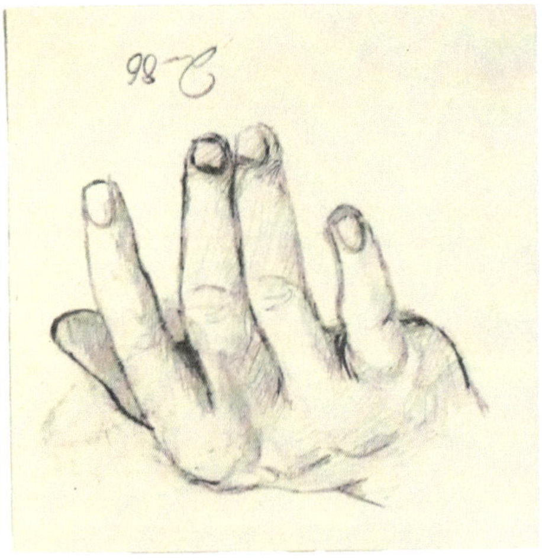

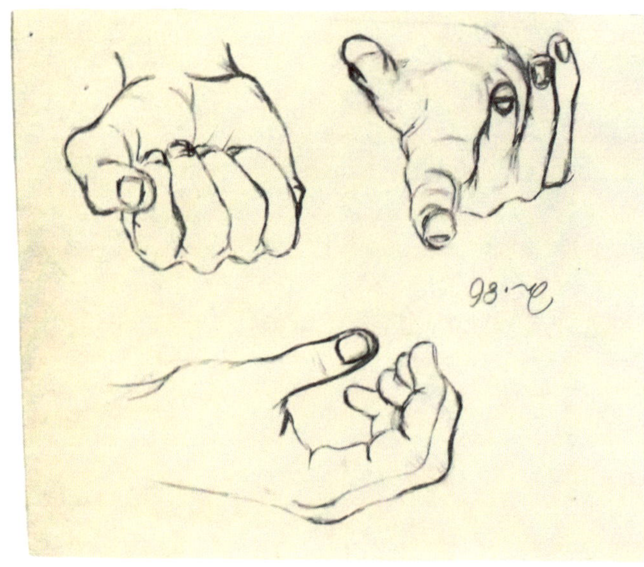

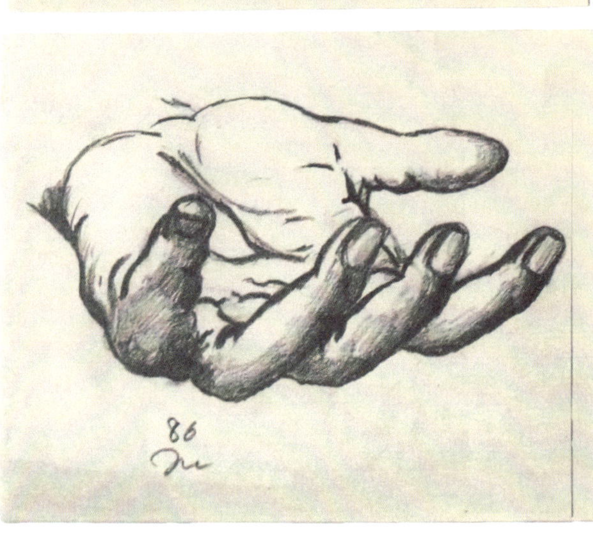
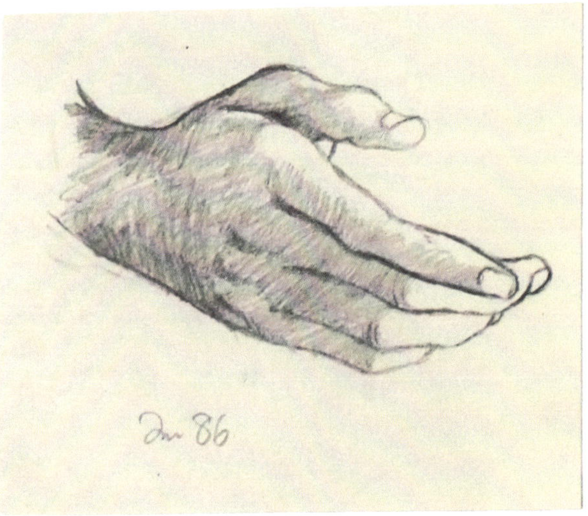
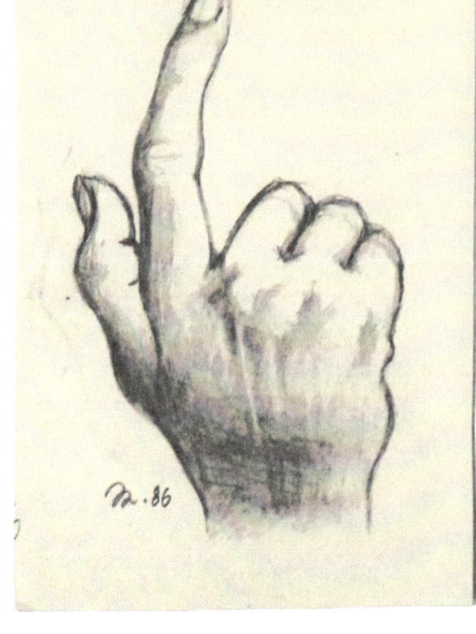
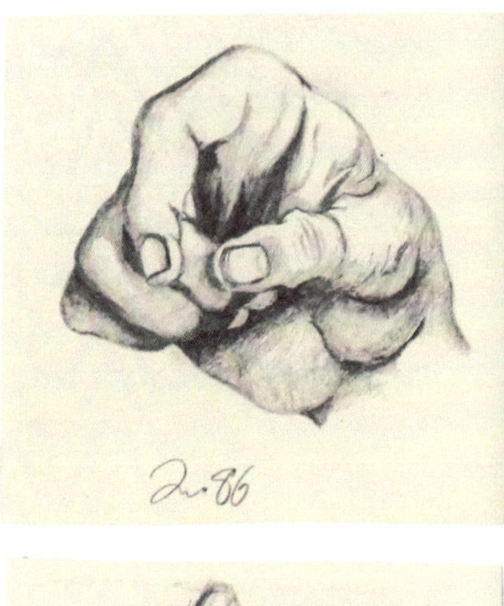

دراسات أيدي، 1989

قلم رصاص على ورق
مقاسات مختلفة
بإذن من الفنان

Studies of Hands, 1989

Graphite on paper
Dimensions variable
Courtesy of the artist

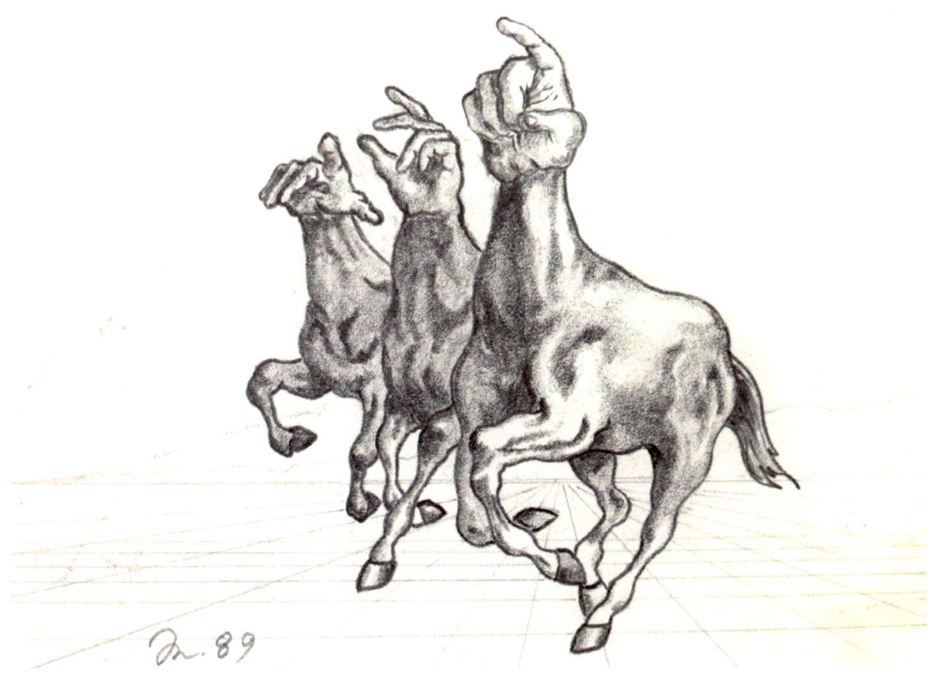

Over There,
preparatory study, 1989

Graphite on paper
15 × 20 cm
Courtesy of the artist

دراسة تحضيرية
لعمل *هناك،* 1989

قلم رصاص على ورق
15 × 20 سم
بإذن من الفنان

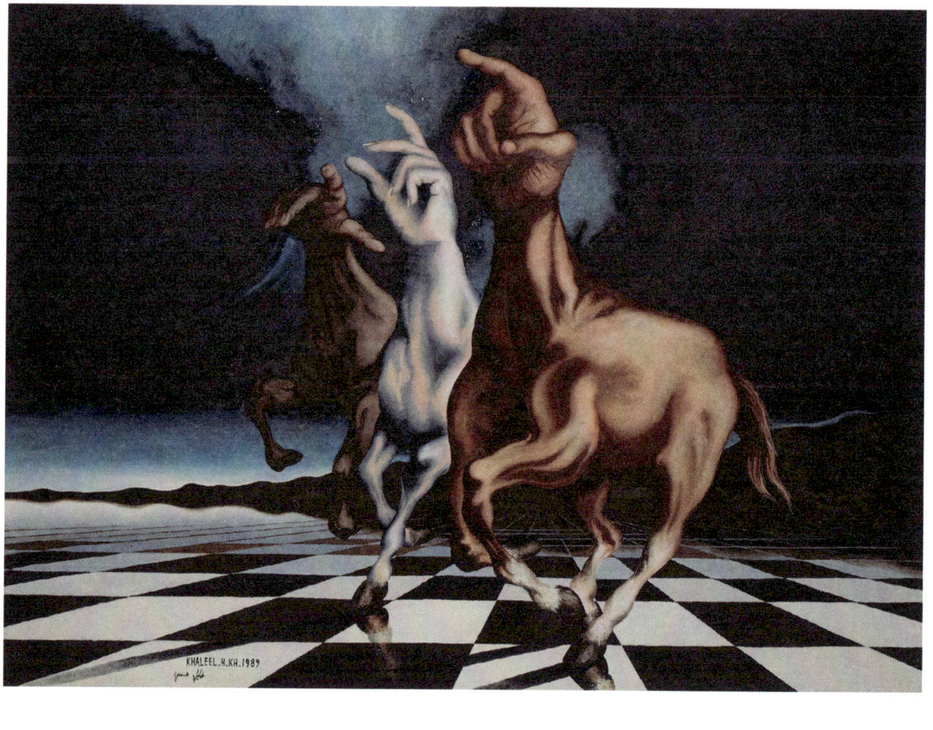

Over There, 1989

Oil on canvas
90 × 120 cm
Courtesy of the artist

هناك، 1989

ألوان زيتية على قماش
120 × 90 سم
بإذن من الفنان

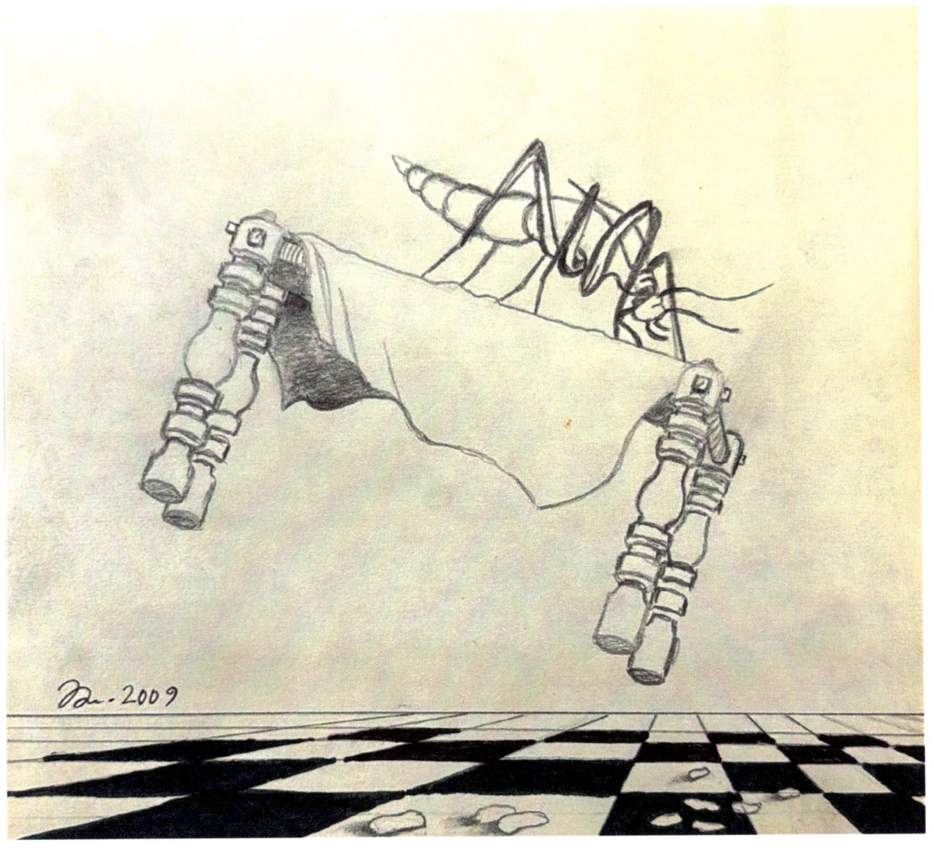

رسمة تحضيرية
لعمل الحمى، 2009

قلم رصاص وحبر على ورق
21 × 19 سم
بإذن من الفنان

Fever,
preparatory drawing, 2009

Graphite and ink on paper
21 × 19 cm
Courtesy of the artist

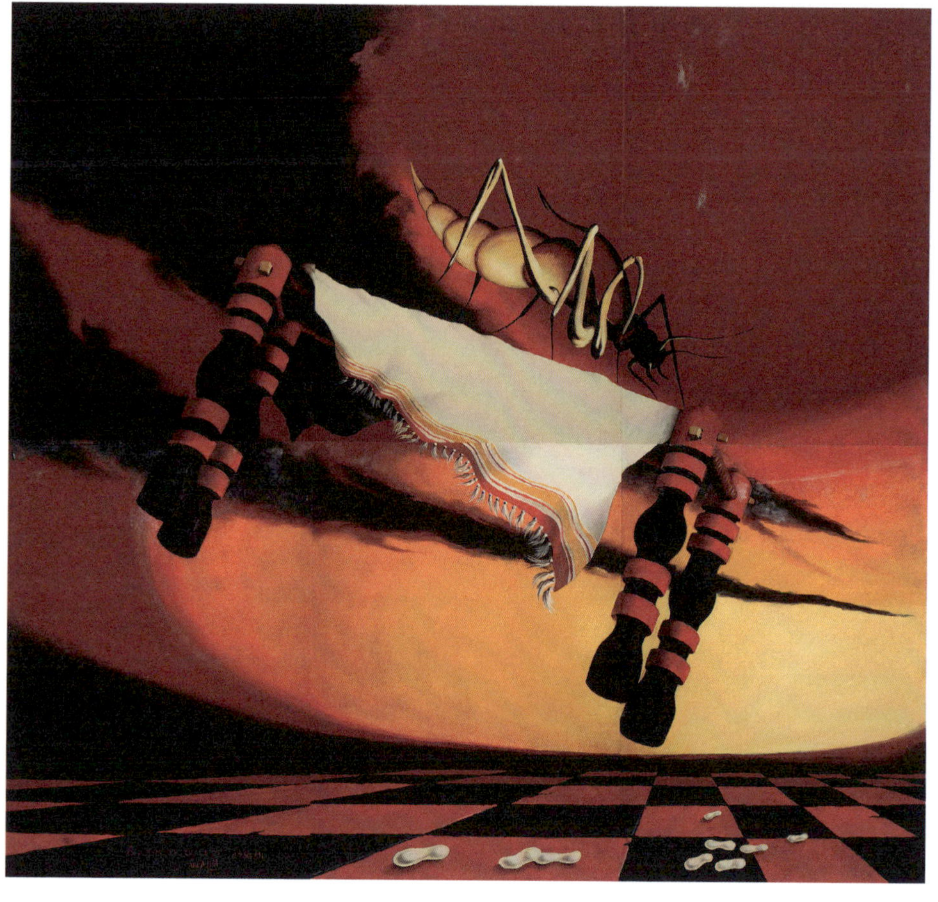

الحمى، 2010

ألوان زيتية على قماش
210 × 200 سم
بإذن من الفنان

Fever, 2010

Oil on canvas
210 × 200 cm
Courtesy of the artist

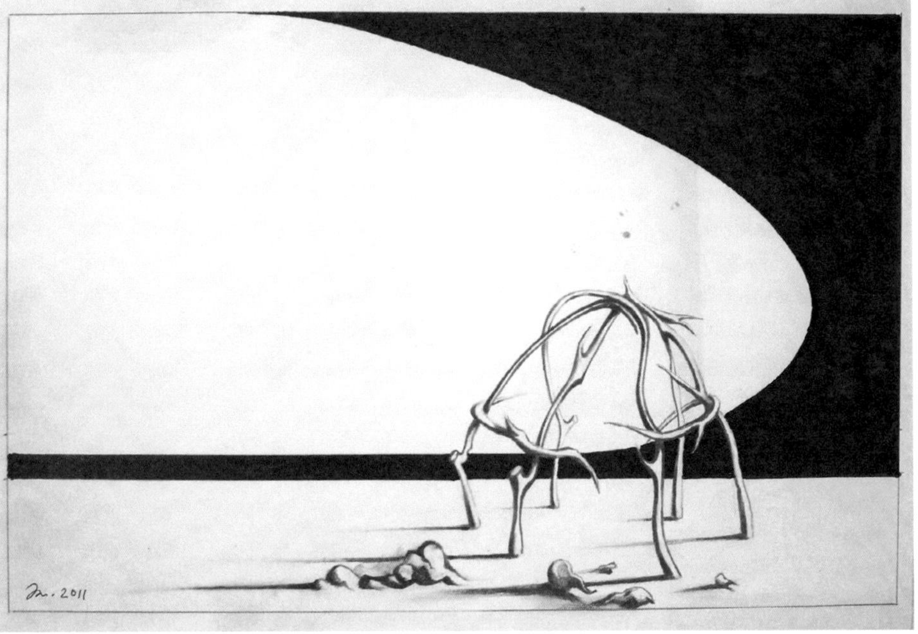

Hunger,
preparatory drawing, 2011

Graphite and ink on paper
21.5 × 31 cm
Courtesy of the artist

رسمة تحضيرية
لعمل الجوع، 2011

قلم رصاص وحبر على ورق
21.5 × 31 سم
بإذن من الفنان

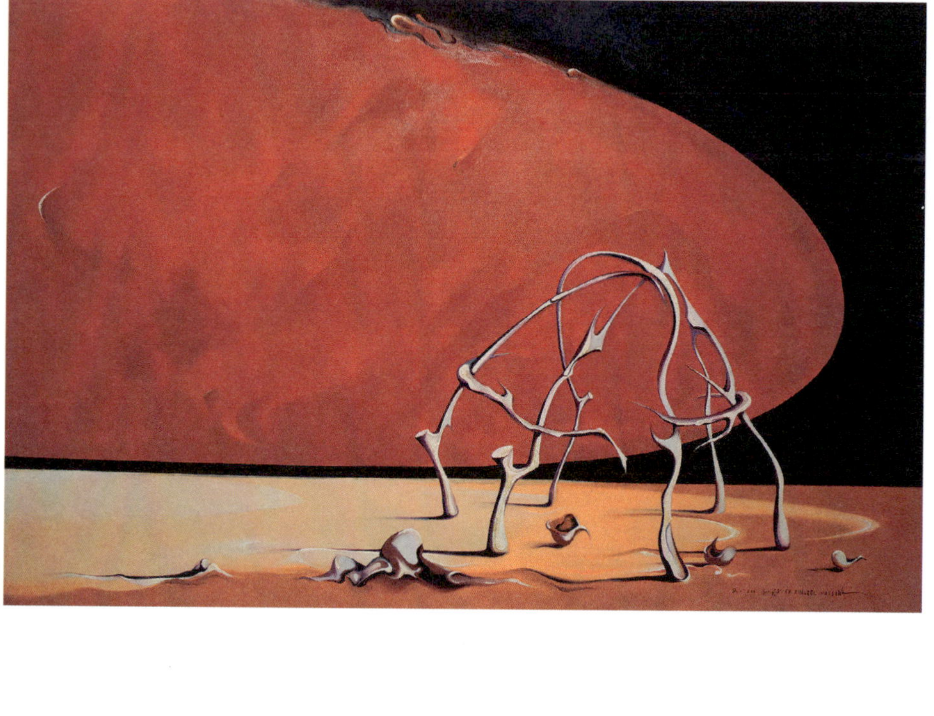

الجوع، 2011

ألوان زيتية على قماش
150 × 100 سم
بإذن من الفنان

Hunger, 2011

Oil on canvas
100 × 150 cm
Courtesy of the artist

الحلم مَنْفَذا إلى الوجدان الجمعي: حلمية خليل حسن خليل

Dream as a Portal to Collective Consciousness: Khaleel Hassan Khaleel's Dreamism

علي المجنوني
Ali Almajnooni

Saudi artist Khaleel Hassan Khaleel has objected on more than one occasion to some principles of Surrealism as it was conceived and practiced in Europe. This can be understood from two angles, the first of which concerns the dilemma that modernism and its outputs across various movements imposed on artists of non-European contexts. Writers and thinkers in the Saudi and broader Arab milieu tackled this problem when they found themselves faced with modernist narratives that were inapplicable to their reality. Compelled to analyze and understand these dilemmas, they arrived at syncretic, constructive resolutions. Some artists, in fact, could not help but question plastic arts and painting in and of themselves as foreign forms of expression, born and developed in other, non-Arab, contexts. It would be no exaggeration to say that some artists remain captive to this incongruity, and at best, they have not found any benefit to glean from it.

The second angle from which we can understand Khaleel's objection to Surrealism is the criticism that the movement has received since its inception in the early twentieth century. In addition to its Eurocentrism

وُثّق عـن الفنـان السـعودي خليـل حسـن خليـل اعتراضُه الـذي عبّر عنه في أكثر من مناسبة على بعض مبادئ السـوريالية كما نشـأت ومُورسـت في أوروبا. ويمكن فهم هذا الاعتراض من جانبين اثنين، أولهمـا المـأزق الـذي طرحتـه الحداثـة ومنتجاتها مـن الحـركات الفنية الحديثـة على الفنانيـن في سـياقات تقع خـارج أوروبا، وهو مـأزق تعامل معه مفكرون وأدبـاء في المشـهد السـعودي على وجه الخصوص، وفي المنطقة العربية بشـكل عام، حين وجدوا أنفسـهم وجها لوجه أمام سـرديات حداثية لا تنطبـق على واقعهـم وتطرح أمامهم مسائل يحتّم عليهـم فهمهـا وتحليلها مـن أجـل إيجـاد حلـول توفيقيـة تمكّنهـم مـن الاسـتفادة منها. بل لم يجـد بعـض الفنانين بُدا مـن أن يواجه تسـاؤلًا عن الفن التشـكيلي ككلّ واللوحة باعتبارهما شـكلين تعبيرييـن أجنبيّيـن في حـد ذاتهما، وُلدا ونشـآ في سـياق آخر مختلف عن السـياق العربي. وليس من المبالغة في شـيء القولٔ إن بعضهم ما زال أسـيرًا لهذا التناقض، وفي أحسـن الأحوال لم يسـتفد منه اسـتفادة إيجابية.

أمـا الجانب الثاني الذي يمكن من خلاله فهمْ اعتـراض خليـل علـى السـوريالية فيكمـن في بعض مـا تعرضت له الحركة من نقـدٍ منـذ ظهورها في

and colonial legacy—evident in its cultural appropriation and failure to acknowledge the sources of some of its aesthetics—Surrealism has been accused of being an elitist movement. Its complex symbolism and reliance on Freudian psychoanalysis has made Surrealist art difficult for the general public to decipher. Its enjoyment, for the most part, has therefore been restricted to an audience of educated elites. Compounding this elitism is the fact that its topics are grounded in philosophical premises and abstract notions, greatly contradicting the movement's aspirations to alter societal consciousness. Even when some Surrealist practices manage to overcome these issues, they are unable to align with the remaining interpretations of the principles of Surrealism. In fact, they clash, signaling the movement's failure to either express coherent political positions or form a cohesive, unified political vision as a necessary foundation to achieve its revolutionary principles.

While several factors underlie this failure, we are concerned in this context about Surrealism's exaggerated focus on the individual and the excessive fascination with dream logic and the unconscious. Surrealism is often accused of escaping reality in lieu of engaging with it and tackling its sociopolitical complexities. In the eyes of some, the movement is based on a self-contained, inward-facing vision that forgoes its outside to forge a secluded domain that is impermeable to the complexities of reality. It thus obscures the human condition and its undergirding societal structure, rather than illuminating and confronting it.

It is through this skeptical lens that one must examine Khaleel's works, artistic practice, and vision, which he has sought to embody in paintings that do not avoid Surrealist aesthetics, despite his stance toward the movement itself. Consistent

مطلـع القرن العشـرين. فبالإضافة إلـى إرث الحركة الاستعماري، المتمثل في اسـتلابها الثقافي وفشلها فـي الاعتـراف ببعـض منابـع جمالياتهـا، إضافـةً إلـى مركزيّتهـا الأوروبيـة، اتُّهمـت السـوريالية بأنها حركـة نخبويـة تصعـب علـى أفهـام عمـوم الناس بسـبب رمزيّتهـا المعقّـدة واعتمادهـا علـى التحليل النفسـي -الفرويـدي-، وهـذا مـا جعـل تـذوق الفن السـوريالي مقصورًا في الغالب علـى قلةٍ من جمهور المتعلميـن، ويضاعف من هذه النخبوية حقيقة أنّ موضوعاتها تنطلق من منطلقات فلسفية ومفاهيم مجـردة، وهـذا الوضـع يتعـارض إلـى درجـة كبيرة مـع مبتغى الحركـة، ألا وهو تغيير وعـي المجتمع. وحتى حين تحـاول بعض الممارسـات السـوريالية تجـاوز هـذا المأزق، فـإن تلك المحـاولات لا تتمكن مـن إحـداث توافـق مـع باقـي التفسـيرات لمبادئ السـوريالية، بـل تتضـارب معهـا، مـا يعنـي إخفاق الحركـة فـي التعبيـر عـن مواقف سياسـية متسـقة وعوزها إلى تشكيل رؤية سياسية مترابطة وموحدة توفّـر الأسـاس الضـروري لتحقيق مبادئهـا الثورية.

وبالطبـع فـإن لهـذا الإخفـاق أسـبابا عـدّة، ولكـن مـا يهمّنا منها في هـذا السـياق مبالغة الفن السـوريالي فـي حصـر نطـاق تركيزه على الفـرديّ، وإفـراط السـوريالية فـي افتتانهـا الشـديد باللاوعي وبمنطـق الأحـلام، إلـى درجـة أنهـا تُتهـم أحيانـا بالهرب من الواقع، وبالاسـتعاضة عـن التعامل مع تعقيـدات الواقـع الاجتماعـي والسياسـي والتعالق معهـا. فالسـوريالية فـي نظـر بعضهـم تقـوم على رؤية جوّانيـة تنعكس إلى الداخل منكفئة على ذاتها مسـتغنية عمـا هـو خارجهـا، تشـيّد مجـالًا منعزلًا ومنيعًا مـن تعقيدات الواقع يفضـي بها إلى تعتيم الوضع الإنسـاني والبنى الاجتماعية التي تسـهم في تشـكيله بدلًا مـن إبرازهـا ومواجهتها.

علـى ضوء هـذا الموقف المتشـكك مـن الفن السـوريالي ينبغـي مقاربة أعمـال خليل وممارسـته الفنيـة ورؤاه التي سـعى إلـى تجسـيدها من خلال لوحـات لا تتفـادى جماليـات الفـن السـوريالي على رغم موقفها من الحركة نفسـها. فبحسـب التحليل

with the psychoanalytic lens on which Surrealism has so greatly relied, dreams are the most prominent channels of the unconscious. Dreams open a window to the unconscious domain and the uncharted regions of the self, providing an exceptional opportunity to seize the creative potential of this illogical, strange, and bizarre world. So, with the loosened grip of logic and consciousness, Surrealists developed writing and artistic techniques that aided the unconscious in surfacing and guiding the creative process.

Khaleel neither entirely accepted these conceptions nor embraced them without scrutiny. On the one hand, he rid the unconscious in Surrealist art from its propensity for individualism, associating it instead with the collective. His paintings do not depict people or topics engrossed in their individualities and centered around themselves. Rather, human presence in his works sheds light on a collective burden grounded in a collective memory and fate. It can be said that Khaleel's redress of Surrealism resembles that of Freudian theory offered by Carl Jung. The Swiss psychologist posited the notion of the collective unconscious, thereby freeing psychoanalysis from its individual-centric constraints while recognizing the collective psychological implications of ancestral influence and cultural transmission, which can help to explain individual and societal behavior.

On the other hand, it can also be said that Khaleel found a compromise in what he termed "Dreamism," wherein "dream" is not a substitute for "reality," but one of its tributaries and, at the same time, an extension of reality. Unfettered by the rules of logic and reason, the dream here is a pliable domain that functions as a beacon to guide the creative, intellectual effort. So, the artist hones in on "panreality," which coalesces once the boundary between dream and reality is dissolved.

النفسـي الذي اعتمدت عليه السوريالية أيّما اعتماد، فإن الأحـلام أكثـر قنـوات اللاوعـي حضـوّرًا فـي الجماليـات السـوريالية. فتحت الأحـلام نافذة علـى مجـال اللاوعـي والمناطـق غير المكتشفة في النفس، ووفرت فرصـة اسـتثنائية لاغتنام الطاقـة الإبداعية لهـذا المجـال اللامنطقـي والغريب والعجيـب، فطـوّر السـورياليون تقنيـات كتابيـة وفنية تسـاعد اللاوعـي علـى الظهـور وتوجيـه العمليـة الإبداعية بعـد تخفيف سـطوة الوعـي والمنطق.

لـم يقبـل خليل بتلـك التصـورات قبـولًا تامًّا، ولـم يعتنقهـا من دون تمحيـص. فمن جهة خلّص اللاوعـي فـي الفـن السـوريالي مـن نزعتـه الفردية وزَبطـه بالجمعيّ. إذ لـم تصور لوحاته أشـخاصًا وموضوعـات منغمسة فـي فردانيتها ومتمركـزة حـول ذاتها، بـل إن الوجود الإنسـاني فيها يسـلط الضـوء علـى هـمّ جمعي أساسـه ذاكـرة مشـتركة ومصيـر مشـترك. وهنـا يمكن القول إن اسـتدراك خليـل فـي ممارسـته السـوريالية يشـبه اسـتدراك كارل يونـغ على نظريـة فرويد، حين قـدم مفهوم اللاوعـي الجمعـي الـذي أخرج بفضله التحليـل النفسـي مـن ربقة التمحـور حـول الفـرد، واعترف بالصبغـة الجمعية للميراث النفسـي والرمزي الذي يفسـر سـلوك الأفـراد والمجتمعات.

ومـن جهـة ثانيـة يمكن القـول إن خليـل قد وجـد حـلًّا توفيقيا فيمـا أسـماه «الحُلميّـة»، فعلى ضوء هذا المذهب لا يكـون الحلم بديلا عن الواقع، وإنما رافـدًا من روافده وامتدادًا له في الآن نفسـه؛ كمـا يكـون الحلـم بمنطقـه المـرن المنفلـت مـن ضوابـط المنطـق وسـطوة العقلانية، غاية تعمل بمثابة فنار يوجّه الجهـد الإبداعي والفكـري، ويركز خليل علـى ما يسـميه «الواقع الأشمل» الذي يتشكل بعـد إذابـة الحـدود بيـن الحلـم والواقع بقصد استكشـاف مناطق تعبيرية جديدة ولكنها ضرورية للتعبيـر عن أحـلام الإنسـان ومخاوفه ومآلاته. وهذا يعني انعدام التضاد بيـن الواقـع والحلـم، ويجعل العالـم الحُلمي الـذي تصوره لوحاتـه بمثابة امتداد عضـوي للواقـع، فالواقـع والحلـم كلاهمـا جزء من

The aim is therefore to discover new expressive domains, which are necessary to elucidate human dreams, fears, and prospects. This entails ending the contradiction between dream and reality, thereby making the dreamist world that he represents in his paintings an organic extension of reality, where both reality and dream are parts of a holistic domain encompassing the human experience. The elements comprising Khaleel's work ultimately intermingle and intertwine organically without repulsing or alienating the viewer.

Sea waves land ashore in the form of human hands delivering paper boats, and the necks of ordinary horses extend as hands as well. Here, Khaleel utilizes the expressive potential of Surrealist art and renders it his own, neither forfeiting individuality nor evading the collective unconscious. His works appear to suggest that he cultivates artistic techniques in new habitats, where the unfamiliar is not rejected but embraced and nurtured until it melds with the terrain. The Surrealist practice is thus released from its enclosure, and a door is opened wide to topics and preoccupations that are closer to nature, more confrontational with reality, increasingly involved with society, and bolder in dealing with the societal structures that shape individual and collective reality.

In his style and approach, Khaleel undoubtedly draws inspiration from how Arab poets and novelists before him have handled literary forms originating in other contexts. They not only utilized those foreign artistic forms to express local cultural and intellectual subject matter, but also offered contributions to global artistic heritage. Even while incorporating an artistic approach to European contextual provenance, Khaleel bent it to topics of his own Arab, Muslim context without finding contradiction or conflict in doing so. Artistic technique here serves conception and vision;

واقـع كلّـي يضم التجربـة الإنسانية، ولهـذا فـإن العناصـر فـي أعمـال خليـل تتجـاور وتتداخـل علـى نحـو عضـوي لا يسـتدعي النفور أو الاسـتغراب.

ينتهي موج البحر عند الشـاطئ بأكفّ بشـرية تحمل قـوارب ورقية، وتمتد رقاب الأحصنة العاديّة علـى هيئة أيـدٍ بشـرية أيضًا. بهذه الطريقة يسـتغل خليـل الإمكانـات التعبيريـة الموجـودة فـي الفـن السـوريالي ويوظفهـا لخدمـة نسـخة خاصـة بـه لا تفرط فـي فردانيتها ولا تنفر مـن اللاوعي الجمعي. تظهـر أعماله وكأنما الفنان يسـتزرع تلـك التقنيات الفنيـة فـي بيئـة جديدة عليهـا، غير أن هـذه البيئة لا ترفـض ما هو غريـب وإنما تحتضنـه وتعينه على النمو حتى يصبح جزءًا منها؛ هكذا تفلت الممارسة السـوريالية من تقوقعها وينفتح البـاب أمامها على مصراعيـه لصالح موضوعات وانشـغالات تكون أكثر التصاقًا بالطبيعة واشتباكًا مع الواقع، وأكثر انخراطًا فـي المجتمع، وأكثر شـجاعة فـي التعامل مع البنى الاجتماعيـة التي تشـكل واقع الفـرد والجماعة، ولا بـدّ أن خليـل اسـتلهم أسـلوبه ومقاربته مما سـبقه إليـه الشـعراء والروائيـون العـرب فـي التعامل مع الأشـكال الأدبية التي نشـأت في سـياقات أخرى، فلم يكتفـوا باسـتخدام الشـكل الفنـي الأجنبـي للتعبير عـن مضاميـن ثقافية وفكرية محليـة فحسـب، وإنمـا تجـاوز إسـهامهم فـي الإرث الفنـي العالمـي مجرد تزويد الشـكل الفني بموضوعـات ومحتويات قادمة مـن أطـراف المركـز الأوروبي. فخليـل، حتى وإن استخدم حركة فنية برزت في السياق الأوروبي، فقد طوّعها لموضوعاته الخاصة التي ترتبط بسـياقه العربـي والإسـلامي، ولـم يجـد فـي ذلـك التطويع تعارضًـا أو تصادمًـا، فالتقنية الفنيـة خادمة للتصور والرؤية، لا تعسـفها أو تقيّدها بحال مـن الأحـوال، لا سـيّما وأن الأدب العربي والتـراث العربيّين غنيّان بمـا يثري الحركة السـوريالية وأسـاليبها في التعامل مـع موضوعاتها.

لقد وجد خليـل الملمـح الثاني للتوفيق بيـن السـوريالية وبيـن الثقافة العربيـة فـي العجيـب والعجائبـي؛ تزخـر المدونـة السـردية العربية

it in no way abuses or restricts them. Arabic literature and Arab heritage can especially enrich the Surrealist movement, including its styles and subject matter.

To reconcile Surrealism with Arab culture, Khaleel found a second feature, namely in the wondrous and the bizarre. The Arabic narrative archive is replete with tales and fables containing elements of the extraordinary and the fantastical, with the sea being an endless source of such stories. Not only does the sea possess precious pearls and rarities in its depths, but it is also home to wondrous creatures that have piqued the Arab imagination and found their way into the collective consciousness. Case in point: *The Wonders of Creation and Curiosities of Existence*, in which the Muslim scholar and geographer Zakariya ibn Mohammed al-Qazwini writes about fishes of strange appearance and behavior populating the Red Sea off the Jizan coast. There, islands uninhabited by humans also harbor unfamiliar, implausible land creatures.

Perhaps Khaleel's *Al-Rawi Said* (2010) contains a clear example of his practice, as even in tackling the abstract concept of time, the painting presents a complex, multilayered treatment, which nevertheless does not depart from the artist's cultural context. It depicts a lone man seated on a chair, legs crossed, against a coffee shop wall. On the table in front of him, a camel caravan is in procession as a giant hand extends downward from outside the frame toward an orange that appears poised to land on the table. In the background, a partially clothed man appears to be dead or on the brink of death. The painting represents time through the material decease that comes as a result of its passage, along which lifetimes end and organic matter perishes. The painting achieves its idea through a manipulation of time, which is evident in multiple facets. Chiefly, the work represents time as a suspended moment, akin to a photographic

بالمرويـات والقصـص التـي تحـوي عناصـر عجائية وفنتازيـة، والبحـر علـى وجـه التحديـد كان مَعينًـا لا ينضـب لهـذه الحكايـات. لا يكتنز البحر فـي أعماقه اللآلـئ والـدرّ الثميـن فحسـب، ولكـن بمخلوقاتـه العجيبـة التـي شـحذت المخيلـة العربيـة ووجدت طريقهـا إلـى الوجـدان العربـي، ففـي كتـاب العالِم والجغرافيّ المسـلم القزوينـي «عجائـب المخلوقات وغرائـب الموجـودات»، فـإن البحـر الأحمـر المطلّ علـى جيـزان مأهـول بأسـماك عجيبـة فـي أوصافهـا وطباعهـا، وبجـزر غير مسـكونة علـى هيئـات دواب ترتبـط بعوالـم قصيّـة تتجاوز المعـروف والمعقول.

ولعـل فـي لوحة «قال الـراوي» (2010م) مثالًا واضحًا علـى ممارسة خليل الفنية، فحتى وهو يعالج مفهومًـا مجـردًا كالزمن نشـهد فـي اللوحـة معالجة معقدة ومتعددة الطبقات لهـذا الموضوع، إلا أنهـا لا تُخرج المعالجة من السياق الثقافي الذي ينتمي إليه الفنان؛ تصوّر اللوحة رجلًا وحيدًا مسـتندًا إلى حائط مقهى يضع إحدى ساقيه فوق الأخرى، وعلى سطح الطاولـة أمامـه تتحرك قافلة مسـافرة مـن الجِمال، بينمـا تتدلـى يـد عملاقـة مـن أعلى اللوحـة في اتجاه برتقالـة معلّقة على وشـك أن تسـقط علـى الطاولة، وفـي خلفية اللوحة رجل نصف عار يبدو ميتا أو على وشـك الموت. تمثّل اللوحة الزمـن من خلال الهلاك المـادي الـذي يجـيء نتيجـة لمـرور الوقـت، فالزمن تفنى فيه الأعمار وتهلك فيه المـادة الحيوية. ولكن العمـل يحقـق فكرتـه بواسـطة التلاعـب بالزمن. في اللوحـة أكثر من وجـه لهـذا التلاعب، أبرزهـا تصوير الزمن عبر لحظة مجمّدة وكأنما بتقنية فوتوغرافية، ومجـاورة لحظتيـن زمنيتيـن مختلفتين. يطغى علـى اللوحة شـعورٌ كثيـف بالترقب، سـببه تجميد لحظة عابـرة وزائلـة تشـحن المشـهد المتوقـف فـي تلك اللحظة. فالبرتقالة التي يغلب الظن أنها أفلتت من اليـد الظاهرة عموديا مـن أعلى اللوحة على وشـك أن تغيّر المشـهد كليا. وثقلها المنتظر على الطاولة يقابلـه ثقـل منتظر في شـحنة مـن التوتـر الدرامي الذي يسـيطر على المشـهد. تصبح طاولـة المقهى، وقافلة الجمال العابرة فوقها، رهنا للفاكهة المعلّقة.

snapshot, while juxtaposing two separate moments in time. A sense of intense anticipation dominates the painting due to the suspension of an ephemeral moment that charges the static scene. The orange, which was presumably released from the vertically extended hand, is about to change the scene entirely. Its anticipated weight upon the table is met with an anticipatory heaviness in the dramatic anxiety that dominates the scene. The transient camel caravan and the coffee shop table on which it treads are at the mercy of the overhanging orange.

The painting also depicts a living body and a lifeless one in the same space, with no conflict between them. This juxtaposition breaks the rules of chronology while concurrently acknowledging them, creating an inner narrative that can be deduced from what exists in the painting itself. The scene points to a certain sequence of events through time, if subtly, by representing distinct moments belonging to one story side by side. This conveys the movement of time and invites the viewer to ponder the different stages of human existence. Though Khaleel does not directly prioritize one event over another, he emphasizes the present by placing it in the fore-ground of the work, where the waiting man occupies the largest portion of the frame. Meanwhile, the partially clothed man lies in the background, as though crawling away from the scene toward a doorway to darkness. The painting acknowledges the linearity of time only to undermine it through this illogical concurrence, where time collapses in a dreamist scenario that resists typical temporal logic.

The theme of temporal change and its impact recurs across Khaleel's works, including in *Human and Machine* (1977), *Face* (1977), and *Face (2)* (1978). Here, Khaleel breaks down his topic into elements that combine the human with the technological or the

أيضًا تُظهـر اللوحـة الجسـد الحـي والجسـد الهالك، فـي فضـاء واحـد لا يتعارضـان فيـه، هـذه المجـاورة تهـدم قوانيـن الزمـن المتسلسـل -الكرونولوجـي- في نفس الوقت الـذي تعترف فيه بهـا، إنها تخلـق سـردية داخليـة يمكن اسـتنباطها ممـا هو موجـود فـي اللوحة نفسـها. إذ تشـير إلى تسلسـل معيـن لأحـداث تقع عبـر الزمـن، حتـى وإن كان تسلسـلًا متقشـفًا، فإنهـا بواسـطة تصويـر لحظـات مختلفة مـن قصة واحدة جنبًا إلى جنب تعبّـر عن حركة الزمـن وتدعو المشـاهد إلـى تأمل مراحل مختلفة من الوجود الإنسـاني، وإن لم يؤكد خليـل تأكيـدًا مباشـرًا علـى أفضلية لحـدث أو آخر فإنـه يبـرز الحاضـر بتقديمـه إلـى واجهـة اللوحة، فالرجـل المنتظـر يتصدر القسـم الأكبر مـن اللوحة بينما الرجل نصف العاري يقبع فـي الخلفية وكأنه يغـادر المشـهد زحفًا إلى البـاب المظلـم. هكذا تقرّ اللوحـة بخطّية الزمن ثم تقوّضهـا، فمن خلال هذا التزامـن اللامنطقـي ينهار الزمن في سـيناريو حُلمّي لا منطقـي يقـاوم المنطـق الزمنـي المعتاد.

تتكـرر ثيمـة تغيّـر الزمـن، والأثر الـذي يحدثه هـذا التغير، في لوحات أخرى لخليل مثل «الإنسـان والآلة» (1977م) ولوحتَـي «وجـه» (1977م و1978م)، حيـث يفكّك خليل موضوع اللّوحة إلى عناصـر تجمع بيـن البشـريّ والتقنيّ أو الآلـيّ معبّرًا عـن انشـغال بطغيـان الآلـة على حسـاب الإنسـان، يعضد هذا الجانب اشـتمال كثير مـن لوحات خليل علـى موتيفـات تتعلـق بمـرور الزمـن وفعلـه، مثل الفاكهة، والبيض، والـدود، والجراد. كمـا أن الفنان كثيرا ما يجـاور الحي بالميت، أو الطـازج بالمتعفن، كمـا نشـاهد فـي لوحة «النهاية» (1977م) التـي تصور مشـهد حطـام لسـفينة يجتمع فيه الطازج من العناصر كطائر الإوز والبيض والميت كعظام السـمك والجماجم البشـرية.

هـذه المعالجـة للزّمـن ترقـى بـه لأن يكـون مفهومًا نظريًـا أو فلسـفيًا طالمـا شـغل المفكرين والفنانيـن، ولكنها أيضًا لا تحـول دون معالجته في سـياق ثقافي مألوف لدى الفنان وجمهوره، والشيء

mechanical, thereby expressing a preoccupation with machine's tyranny over man. This aspect is reinforced by the inclusion in the artist's paintings of various motifs related to the passage and impact of time, such as fruit, eggs, worms, and locusts. He often juxtaposes the living and the dead or the pristine and the decaying, as seen in *The End* (1977), where a scene depicting the bare hull of a crashed ship combines the pristine (a goose and an egg) with decay (a fish skeleton and human skulls).

Khaleel thus elevates time as a theoretical or philosophical concept that has long preoccupied thinkers and artists, but he does not forgo treating it in a cultural context familiar to his audience. The same applies to other concepts that the artist presents using borrowed visual motifs, as he has employed what can be seen as visual loans or archetypes for the treatment of certain ideas or concepts. A prime example is *Door* (1979), where natural, human, and synthetic elements are depicted in exaggerated dimensional disproportion to one another. In the scene, a woman, who is given sufficient though minimal features, appears taller than a wooden door whose existence is rendered futile as it stands in the wilderness. While it is possible to find the links between the painting's three elements, the composition is subject to the concept that Khaleel seeks to put forward. The same can be said about *Desire* (1981) (fig. 1), where the head of a tiger baring its fangs emerges from the background. The threatening creature averts attention away from a dining table on which a platter bearing fish, fruit, and vegetables is centered in a composition dominated by the color red. With this particular feature—whereby paintings are approximations of visual metaphors that are used to explore abstract concepts—Khaleel is reminiscent of Belgian artist René Magritte, whose paintings deal with specific psychological concepts.

نفسه ينطبق على مفاهيم أخرى استخدم فيها خليل استعارات بصرية لتقديمها، إذ يمكن النظر إلى كثير من لوحات خليل على أنها استعارات أو مجازات بصرية مسخّرة لمعالجة فكرة أو مفهوم معين، وليس أدلّ على ذلك من لوحة «باب» (1979م)، على سبيل المثال، فهي تصور أحجام مبالغ فيها لعناصر طبيعية وبشرية وصناعية لا تتوافق فيما بينها، فالمرأة التي أعطيت من الملامح ما هو كافٍ ومقتصدٍ في الوقت نفسه، تبدو أطول من الباب الخشبي، والباب المنتصب في العراء يجعل من فكرة وجوده شيئا عبثيا، وإن كان من السهل إيجاد الصلات بين عناصر اللوحة الثلاثة، لكن التكوين ككلّ خاضع للمفهوم الذي يسعى خليل إلى طرحه. والشيء نفسه يمكن أن يقال عن لوحة «الرغبة» (1981م) (شكل 1)، حيث يظهر من الخلفية المعتمة رأسٌ لنمرٍ مكشّر عن أنيابه، ويسرق الاهتمام من سفرة طعام يتوسطها طبق من السمك وبعض الخضار والفاكهة في تكوين يغلب عليه اللون الأحمر. وخليل في هذا الملمح تحديدًا، ملمح أن تكون اللّوحات تقريبًا مرادفًا لمجازات بصرية تستخدم لاستكشاف مفاهيم مجردة، يشبه في هذا الفنان البلجيكي رينيه ماغريت الذي تعالج لوحاته مفاهيم سايكولوجية محددة.

أخيرًا تأتي نسخة خليل حسن خليل من السوريالية -أو الحلمية كما يسميها- متجذرة في التاريخ الثقافي للمنطقة ومتعالقة مع المحيط الذي نشأ فيه ومرتبطة ارتباطًا عضويًا بالطبيعة. تستقي ممارسته الفنية رؤيتها للحياة من الإرث الثقافي العربي من دون اصطدام بقيم المجتمع ومُثُله أو الدخول في مواجهة عدائية مع الأعراف السائدة فيه. إنها باختصار ليست معنيّة بنزع السيطرة التي يمارسها العقل والمنطق على الحياة أو تغييب تلك السيطرة عن التجربة الإنسانية. في ظل هذه التصورات تبرز أهمية الفنان خليل حسن خليل باعتباره واحدًا من الفنانين الذين استطاعوا التفاعل مع المشهد الفني العالمي والإسهام فيه،

Khaleel's form of Surrealism, or "Dreamism" as he calls it, is rooted in the region's cultural history. Intertwined with the environment of his upbringing, his style is organically linked to nature. His artistic practice and outlook on life are further nourished by his Arab cultural heritage; they neither clash with societal values and ideals nor antagonize prevailing customs. In short, his practice is not interested in wresting control over life from mind and logic or isolating it from the human experience. It is amid these conceptualizations that the significance of Khaleel Hassan Khaleel is brought to the fore. As an artist, he interacts with and contributes to the global art scene by absorbing the influence of world-spanning artistic perspectives and concepts. He then reorients them in step with local culture, along with historical, geographic, and cultural contexts that differ markedly from the context from which they emerged. His practice is sure of itself and open to others, interacting with international artistic currents without losing its link to an ancient Arab culture that still contributes to world literature and art.

من خـلال التأثر برؤى فنية وتصورات عالمية وإعادة صياغتها بما يتناسـب مـع ثقافة محلية في سـياق تاريخـي وجغرافـي وثقافـي يختلـف اختلافـا بيّنًـا عن السـياق الـذي ولـدت فيه. إنها معتـدّة بذاتها ومنفتحـة على الآخر، تتفاعل مـع الاتجاهات الفنية العالمية مـن دون أن تفقد صلتهـا بالثقافة العربية الضاربة فـي القِدم، والتي ما تزال تسـهم في الأدب والفـن العالميّين.

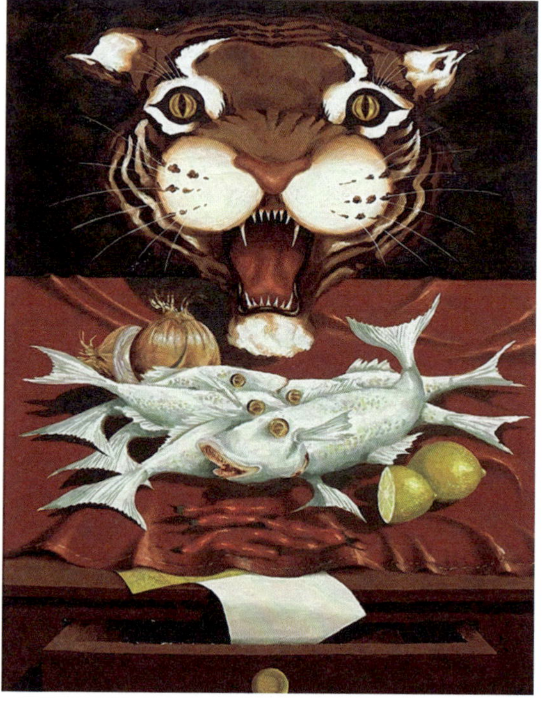

fig. 1   شكل 1

The Whisper of Dreams
Khaleel Hassan Khaleel

April 23–September 25, 2025

Prince Faisal bin Fahd Arts Hall

Riyadh, Saudi Arabia

Curators

Cecilia Ruggeri, Curator at Misk Art Institute

Shadin Albulaihed, Assistant Curator
at Misk Art Institute

Art Direction

Amerah Altufail, Art Production Director
at Misk Art Institute

Exhibition Designers

Alanood Alkhaldi, Exhibition Designer
at Misk Art Institute

Badr Zabarah, Senior Exhibition Designer
at Misk Art Institute

Translations

Moussa Alhouchi

Omar Odeh

Authors

Cecilia Ruggeri

Shadin Albulaihed

Ali Almajnooni

Basma Alshathry, Director of Curatorial
Department and Chief Curator

Copyediting

Abdulrahman Sidi, Senior Editor
at Misk Art Institute

Eti Bonn-Muller

Special thanks to the artist and collector Mohammed Alalyani
for their invaluable contributions.

قد سمعنا ما قلت في الأحلام
خليل حسن خليل

ابريل 23- سبتمبر 25، 2025

صالة الأمير فيصل بن فهد للفنون

الرياض، المملكة العربية السعودية

القيّم الفني

سيسيليا روجيري، قيم فني في معهد مسك للفنون

شادن البليهد، قيم فني مساعد
في معهد مسك للفنون

التوجه الإبداعي

أميرة الطفيل، مدير الإخراج الفني
في معهد مسك للفنون

تصميم المعرض

العنود الخالدي، مصمم المعارض
في معهد مسك للفنون

بدر زباره، مصمم أول للمعارض
في معهد مسك للفنون

الترجمة

موسى الحوشي

عمر عودة

المؤلفون

سيسيليا روجيري

شادن البليهد

علي المجنوني

بسمه الشثري، مدير عام إدارة التقييم الفني
وكبير القيمين الفنيين

التدقيق اللغوي

عبدالرحمن سيدي، محرر أول
في معهد مسك للفنون

إيتي بون مولر

شكر خاص للفنان والمقتني محمد العلياني على مساهماتهم القيمة

Book Design and Layout
-scope Ateliers

English Proofreading
Zeina Assaf

First edition, 2025
© Kaph Books, 2025
© Misk Art Institute, 2025

ISBN: 978-614-8035-76-0

Printed in April 2025

Published by

ꓘAPH
ART BOOKS FROM THE ARAB WORLD
كتـب الفـن مـن العالـم العربـي

www.kaphbooks.com

Distribution
NORTH AMERICA - LATIN AMERICA - ASIA - AUSTRALIA
ARTBOOK | D.A.P.
75 Broad Street, Suite 630
New York, NY 10004
www.artbook.com

FRANCE - SWITZERLAND - BELGIUM - LUXEMBOURG
Les Presses du Réel
35 rue Colson,
21000 Dijon, France
www.lespressesdureel.com

REST OF EUROPE
Idea Books
Nieuwe Herengracht 11
1011 RK Amsterdam, The Netherlands
www.ideabooks.nl

MIDDLE EAST
CIEL BOOK DISTRIBUTION
Al Manara Road, Al Quoz 1, P.O.Box 282005
Dubai United Arab Emirates
www.ciel.me

تصميم الكتاب وتنسيقه
-سكوب أتلييه

المراجعة اللغوية العربية
محمد حمدان

جميع الحقوق محفوظة. يُحظر استنساخ هذا المنشور كلياً أو جزئياً، بأي شكل من الأشكال باستخدام الوسائل الإلكترونية أو الميكانيكية أو غيرها، بما في ذلك النسخ أو التسجيل أو في أي نظام لتخزين أو استرجاع المعلومات، دون الحصول على موافقة مسبقة من الناشر ومعهد مسك للفنون.

الطبعة الأولى، 2025
© كتب كاف، 2025
© معهد مسك للفنون، 2025

ردمك: 978-614-8035-76-0

طُبع في نيسان 2025

النشر من قبل

ꓘAPH
ART BOOKS FROM THE ARAB WORLD
كتـب الفـن مـن العالـم العربـي

www.kaphbooks.com

التوزيع
أمريكا الشمالية - أمريكا اللاتينية - آسيا - أستراليا
ARTBOOK | D.A.P.
75 شارع برود، جناح 630
نيويورك، نيويورك 10004
www.artbook.com

فرنسا - سويسرا - بلجيكا - لوكسمبورغ
Les Presses du Réel
35 شارع كولسون،
21000 ديجون، فرنسا
www.lespressesdureel.com

بقية أوروبا
Idea Books
نيووي هيرنغراخت 11
RK 1011 أمستردام، هولندا
www.ideabooks.nl

الشرق الأوسط
CIEL BOOK DISTRIBUTION
شارع المنارة، القوز 1، ص.ب 282005
دبي، الإمارات العربية المتحدة
www.ciel.me